Learning to Read for Teens Part Two
A Remedial Reading Program
With Science Interwoven Within the Narratives

Teacher/Student Edition

Daniel Langer

Copyright by Daniel Langer
July, 1999
Revised November, 2021

Dan7L.dan@gmail.com

Table of Contents

Teacher's Introduction

Word List 1: On the Beach at Night
Skills: contractions, -er/-ar, -y/-ly.
Concepts: Astronomy: Big Bang Theory; relative size of heavenly bodies, distance of sun and moon from earth, light year; solar eclipse, lunar eclipse.

WORD LIST 2: Ugly Snaps
Skills: contractions, -tion, per-
Concepts: Evaporation, perspiration.

WORD LIST 3: Lips of Honey
Skills: contractions, -tion, hu = /yu/
Concepts: Solids, liquids, and gases; condensation, humidity.

WORD LIST 4: Hector Gets a Job
Skills: -ule, -ful, -ous, -ious
Concepts: Molecules in solids, liquids and gases; heat, melting, freezing.

WORD LIST 5: Hector Goes to Flame's Apartment
Skills: c=k; c=s: ci, ce, cy
Concepts: Cells: nucleus, cytoplasm, cell membrane; concept of cell division; cigarettes and cancer; sun block.

WORD LIST #6: Photographs on the Beach
Skills: ph, sph, tch, plurals with es
Concepts: Amphibians, reptiles, mammals, day, night, month, year, lunar phases, seasons

WORD LIST #7: Hector Gets a Date with Flame and Ann
Skills: com-, con-, ch = k, -ium, -ble, 2- syllable double vowels
Concepts: Introduction to concepts needed to understand digestion, circulation, and respiration; sugar, vitamins and minerals; diagram of cell, mitochondria; elements, atoms, compounds; tests for oxygen, hydrogen, and carbon dioxide; burning magnesium.

WORD LIST #8: A Vicious Fight at the Concert
Skills: sion = tion, sion = zjun, -cious, eu = /oo/
Concepts: Atom; electricity, electric charge, electromagnets, electromagnetic sectrum and wavelengths, television and radio waves; danger of playing with chemicals; anatomy and function of the eye.

WORD LIST #9: The Patient
Skills: -age, -ent, -ant, -ual, -ture, -cial, -tial, -cient, -tient
Concepts: Electric shock to restore heartbeat; voltage, resistance, current, series circuit, parallel circuit; corneal transplant; transparent, translucent, opaque; anatomy and function of flower; liver; kidney.

Learning to Read for Teens Part Two
A Remedial Reading Program
With Science Interwoven Within the Narratives

Teacher's Guide

The aim of this book is to teach basic science concepts along with remedial reading skills, using high interest stories geared to city teens and pre-teens. The ability to decode difficult words is essential to the comprehension of any science text. Reading words in word families and spelling these words from dictation is an effective technique for improving decoding skills. If a student can spell a word, he or she can read the word.

As a teacher of remedial reading and science in special and regular education for over thirty years, I have learned that poor decoding skills and a weak vocabulary are significant impediments to reading science texts or other academic contexts. Even when the student succeeds in struggling through the decoding and the vocabulary, he often finds the content unrelated to his life.

To address this issue, the stories run like a teenage soap opera, with boy/girl relationships, adolescent humor, and conflict resolution. Story lines continue from one story into the next, often ending in cliffhangers that entice the student into wanting to read more. Mixed into each story is significant science content that is related to the lives of the characters. In addition, care has been taken to teach health consciousness, social skills, and values. The Application of scientific knowledge to everyday situations will become apparent to each student.

At the same time, the stories are designed to teach linguistic decoding skills. A list of words for decoding, spelling, and vocabulary building introduces each story. These word lists target fourth through six grade reading levels.[1] The word lists are not meant to be all-inclusive, but to remediate gaps in the secondary student's decoding ability. Each word list covers a few basic word patterns based on the science words needed for the content. Other words having the same linguistic pattern are added to the list.

The word lists should be read aloud with help from the teacher. If the students have difficulty reading the word lists, the teacher should dictate words from the list for the students to write, including short sentences. If the student succeeds in spelling a word, he will have far less difficulty decoding the word when he or she sees it in the story. Spelling the words in word families makes spelling success more likely. If the student can transfer sounds to letters and spell a word, he or she will be able to read the word. When a student gets stuck on one of these words while reading, the student should look at it and spell it.

---

[1] Lower level decoding skills are taught *in Learning to Read for Teens, a Reading Program for the Teenage Student*. Students having difficulty decoding words having short and long vowels sounds should work with *Learning to Read for Teens* first, with stories using the same characters and word family techniques as *The Cool Science Reader*. This book works very well with learning disabled adolescent students reading at a second to third grade reading level.

Often just spelling the word in the text will be enough to enable the student to read it. Large science words will become more familiar and less anxiety provoking.

Every word in each word list is included in the story that follows. The students should read and discuss the stories in groups. For students having significant decoding problems, reading aloud to each other in small groups and giving each other brief spelling tests from the word lists is highly effective.

The questions at the end of each story test reading comprehension skills and give the students an opportunity to express basic science concepts in writing. Scientific concepts and issues raised in the stories should be discussed in class.

The stories are aimed at learning science concepts, while building decoding skills at the same time. Students going through this program will come out with improved decoding skills and vocabulary — including scientific vocabulary — as well as a broadened background in general science concepts, corresponding to sixth through eighth grade New York State science curricula in physical sciences, life sciences, and earth sciences. Contextual clues often help the young reader determine the meaning of new vocabulary words. Scientific concepts are stated by the characters or taught through the context of the stories. The increased understanding of general science concepts will be important in tackling more difficult scientific texts. The ability to decode the word on the page is critical, and background knowledge is essential to comprehension.

This book continues the stories with the same characters from *Learning to Read for Teens*. In *Learning to Read for Teens*, reading phonemes start from the very beginning — *bat, fat, cat*. That book is designed for the teenage reader who has not mastered basic decoding skills, and is reading at a first to third grade level. Students at a second to third grade level can skip the opening word lists and just read quickly through the opening stories. The present volume, *The Cool Science Reader*, builds upon basic decoding skills, concentrating on more difficult phonemes and multisyllabic words, along with reading in the science content area.

Student's Edition **WORD LIST #1** (contractions, -ight, -er, -ar, -y, -ly) © **Daniel Langer**

	A	B	C
1	don't = do not	dark	big ger
2	didn't = did not	Mars	smal ler
3	can't = can not	stars	larg er
4	that's = that is	polestar	sum mer
5	what's = what is	scar	clo ser
6	there's = there is	so lar	bet ter
7	it's = it is	lu nar	sil ver
8	I'll = I will	po lar	dip per
9	I'm = I am	tar tar	Big Dip per
10	you'll = you will	reg u lar	strong er
11	you've = you have	mus cu lar	bright er
12	let's = let us	cir cu lar	to geth er
13	you're = you are	rec tang u lar	Ju pit er
14	we're = we are	ti ny	di am e ter
	they're = they are	ug ly	Ve nus
15	wouldn't = would not	chil ly	plan et
16	couldn't = could not	smel ly	re flects
17	light	real ly	re flect ed
18	right	bright ly	re volve
19	sight	u su al ly	re volves
20	fight	nat u ral ly	re volved
21	bright	grav i ty	e volved
22	night	at oms	grav i ta tion
23	tonight	Po lar is	grav i ta tion al
24	starlight	dis ap pear	lun a tic
25	moonlight	e clipse	at trac tion
26	daylight	u ni verse	ex plo ded
27	sunlight	light year	nav i gate
			con stel la tion

For Reading Only

shoulder	theory
science	distance
scientists	explosion
mystery	guitar

8

Story #1 (contractions, -ight, -er, -ar, -y, -ly) © **Daniel Langer**
Concepts: astronomy

On the Beach at Night

Hector sat down next to Ann. Their friends, Nat and Kate, were already sitting on the other end of their blanket that lay on the sand at Orchard Beach. It had been a warm summer day, but as the sun began to set, a cool breeze blew in from the water.

"It's getting chilly," said Ann.

Hector put his muscular arm around Ann. "I'll keep you warm," he said.

"Your arm feels nice around me," Ann said, as she looked at the water.

Nat put his thin arm around Kate's shoulder. "I don't want you to get cold," Nat said.

As the sun set, it turned a bright orange.

"The sun looks big, now," said Kate. "It looks close enough to touch."

"Yeah," said Hector. "It looks like a big orange basketball."

"How could a ball so small give off so much light?" asked Ann.

"The sun is much bigger than the earth," said Nat. "A hundred earths could fit in a straight line across the diameter of the sun. It would take a million earths to fill up the sun."

"Then why does the sun look like the size of my basketball?" asked Hector, as he sat a little closer to Ann.

"The sun is far away," said Kate.

"That's right," said Nat. "The sun looks small because it is 93,000,000 miles away from the earth."

As the sun set in the western sky, a full silver moon appeared in the east.

"The moon looks the same size as the sun," said Ann.

"The moon is much smaller than the earth," said Nat.

"During a solar eclipse, the moon moves in front of the sun and blocks the sunlight, making a shadow on the earth," said Kate. "How can the moon block out the sun if the moon is so much smaller than the sun?"

"The moon is much closer to the earth than the sun," said Nat. "The moon is only about 240,000 miles from the earth, and the sun is 93,000,000 miles away. During an eclipse, the smaller moon can block the larger sun because the moon is much closer to the earth."

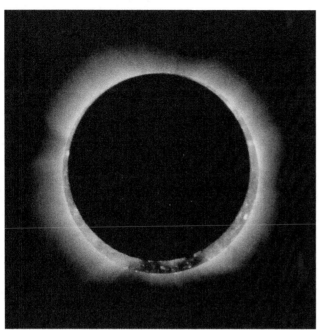
Photo of solar eclipse: Moon is blocking the sun.

"OK," said Ann. "A solar eclipse is when the moon blocks the sun. During a solar eclipse, the sun seems to disappear and the sky gets dark. Then what is a lunar eclipse?"

"That's easy," said Hector. "Lunar is like the Spanish word for moon. During a lunar eclipse, the moon seems to disappear."

"Hey, Hector, you're not as dumb as you look," said Nat. "A lunar eclipse occurs at night, when the moon passes through the earth's shadow."

"Who are you calling dumb?" said Hector, who was looking hard at Nat. "You're so skinny, when you turn sideways, *you* disappear."

"And you're so muscular," Nat replied, "you do pushups with your brain."

"OK, boys," said Ann. "Cool it, or we're going home."

"Don't worry, we were only kidding around," said Nat.

"Hey," said Hector, who was holding his thumb up to the moon. "If I close one eye, I can block out the moon out with my thumb. My thumb is small, but since it is so close to my eye, my thumb can block out the moon!"

"The moon is small," said Ann, "but since it is so much closer to us than the sun, the moon can block out the sun. During a solar eclipse, the moon gets between us and the sun, and makes a shadow on the earth."

"The moon may be smaller than the earth," added Nat, "but it's not tiny. The moon is as wide as the United States."

Solar Eclipse
From parts of the earth, the moon blocks the view of the sun.

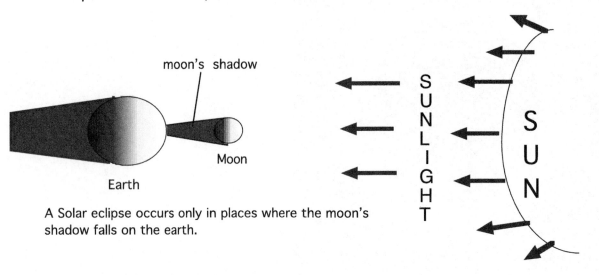

A Solar eclipse occurs only in places where the moon's shadow falls on the earth.

Lunar Eclipse
The moon crosses the earth's shadow

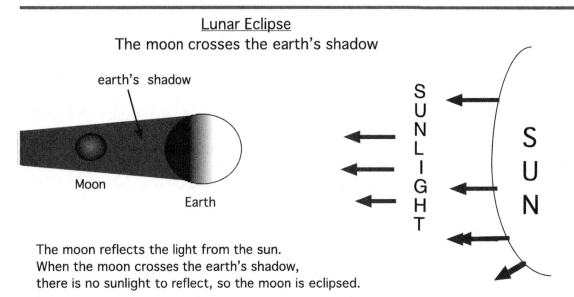

The moon reflects the light from the sun.
When the moon crosses the earth's shadow,
there is no sunlight to reflect, so the moon is eclipsed.

It was getting dark now, and the stars were beginning to appear in the sky. Hector held his left thumb in the air, blocking the moonlight from his eye. Hector's right hand was around Ann's shoulder. Hector moved his left thumb from the air onto Ann's cheek. He gently moved her face towards his and tried to give Ann a kiss.

"Stop it," said Ann. "I did not come to the beach to make out."

"But the stars are out, and there's a full moon tonight!" Hector said. "You look so cute in the moonlight under the stars! Just one kiss!" Hector tried to kiss Ann on her lips, but Ann turned her head, and he kissed her on the ear.

"Try that again," said Ann, "and I'll slap you so hard you'll see stars in daylight!"

"Cut it out," said Kate. "Just look at those stars! They look so tiny!"

"Stars may look small," said Nat, "but they're much bigger than the earth."

"They are?"

"Most of those stars are just as big as our sun, many are even bigger. The sun is just an average sized star."

"If the sun is just a regular star, then why do stars look so small?" asked Ann.

"Stars are many light years away," said Nat.

"Light years away?" asked Kate. "I don't understand. How much time is a light year?"

"Let me explain," said Nat. "A light year is not a measure of *time*. A light year is a measure of *distance* — the distance light travels in a year. Light travels really fast — 186,000 miles in one second. Light from the moon takes about two *seconds* to reach us. Light from the sun takes about eight *minutes* to reach the earth. Light from the stars takes *years* to reach us. Some stars are hundreds of light years away."

"Wait a second," said Hector. "If it takes years for starlight to reach us, then when we look at a star, we don't see the star the way it is today, but the way it was when its light first left the star. If a star is 500 light years away, then we are seeing light that left the star 500 years ago, when Columbus sailed for America! That's like looking into the past!"

"I never thought of it that way," said Nat, "but, you're right. Starlight is old news. Some of the stars we are looking at tonight may have exploded years ago."

"Well, getting back to the here and now, it's really getting chilly," said Kate.

Nat rubbed his hands on Kate's back. "Is that better?" he asked.

"A little," said Kate, "but I'm still cold."

"Let's sit closer together and put the beach blanket around our shoulders," said Ann. The four sat close together wrapped in the beach blanket. It was really dark, now, and the stars over the dark ocean were shining brightly.

"Look at those stars over there!" Nat said, pointing to the dark sky. "That's the Big Dipper!"

"Where?" asked Kate.

"Over there," said Nat, leaning closer to Kate. "Four stars with a rectangular shape make the cup of the dipper, with three stars forming the handle."

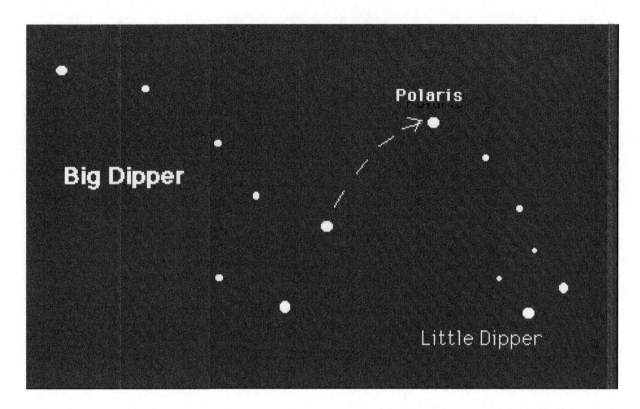

"Oh yes!" said Kate. "I see them! It's like playing connect-the-dots to form a picture. I just saw my first constellation! I read about them in my science book."

"And look over there," said Nat. "That's the little dipper. See the star at the end of the Little Dipper's handle? That's the polestar, Polaris. The polestar is always above the north pole."

"So that's how Columbus knew which way he was going at night!" said Ann. "The polestar told him which way was north."

"You've got it," said Nat. "Polaris is used by sailors to navigate at night."

"Where did all those stars come from?" asked Ann. "Where did everything in the universe come from?"

"Scientists believe it all began with the Big Bang," said Nat.

"The Big Bang?" asked Ann. "What's that?"

"The Big Bang Theory says that the universe began as a tiny speck that exploded — an explosion of light. The Big Bang was not only the beginning of the universe: it was also the beginning of *time*. From that light came the first atoms. Gravity pulled the atoms together to form the first stars."

"Where did the Big Bang come from?" asked Ann.

"Nobody knows," said Nat.

"I thought God made the universe," said Kate.

"Maybe that's how God got the universe started — with a big bang," said Ann.

"Could be," said Nat. "I just don't know, but once it got started, the laws of the universe took over, and everything evolved naturally. Things developed on their own according to the laws of nature."

"Well, I can't see how it could start up all by itself," said Kate. "And where did the laws of the universe come from? Why is there a law of gravity? In a universe without gravity, there wouldn't be anything to hold the stars together."

"That's right," said, Nat. "Stars are balls of gas. The gases are held together by gravity. Without gravity, you couldn't have stars. I don't know why there is a law of gravity. That's just the way it is. Gravity was there at the start of the Big Bang. I don't know how. It's just there."

"Well, I think God made it that way," said Kate.

"Could be," said Nat. "Science can't tell us why there are laws like the law of gravity."

"Or what keeps the law of gravity going," Kate added.

"I know one thing," said Hector. "I have an attraction towards Ann that is stronger than gravity. It is stronger than the gravitational pull between Venus and Mars"

"Well, don't pull me any closer," said Ann. "You're making me feel like I'm on the planet Jupiter."

"Jupiter is a big planet," said Nat. "Big planets have strong gravity. My attraction towards Kate is as strong as the gravitational pull of Jupiter."

"Look!" said Nat, pointing to the sky. "I think that's the planet Jupiter!"

"Planets are usually brighter than stars because planets are much closer to us," said Kate.

"What's the difference between a planet and a star?" asked Ann.

"Stars give off their own light, just as the sun does. The sun is a star. Planets reflect the light of the sun, just the way the moon does. The earth is a planet. Planets revolve around the sun."

"Revolve?" asked Kate.

"Revolve — move around and around another object," said Ann. "The planets revolve around the sun in a circular path. The moon revolves around the earth."

"Not an exact circle," said Nat. "But you have the idea."

"And my heart revolves around you, Ann," said Hector looking into Ann's eyes. "Your eyes are like starlight. You are like a star, and I am like a planet. My life revolves around you, and any light that I have is really your light reflected in me."

"Hector," kidded Nat, "your head is as round as a planet. Light bounces off it the way the moon reflects sunlight. Big Bubba thought your head was a basketball. He shot it at the basket, and your head revolved around the rim so many times that you still can't stop feeling dizzy."

"You snap on me one more time," said Hector, "and my fist will will show your flat head what the Big Bang was really like! You will be left with an ugly scar to match your ugly face!"

"Say it with your mouth closed," said Nat. "The smelly tartar on your teeth is as yellow as the moon."

"I wouldn't talk," said Hector. "You're the most popular kid in the gym. Everyone wants to use your head as a ball."

"Cool it, boys," said Ann. "We didn't come out here to fight."

"I'll cool it," said Hector, "only if I can get a kiss from your warm lips."

"If you think I'm going to kiss you to get you to stop acting like a lunatic," said Ann, "then you must be from another planet!"

"Hey!" said Nat. "I just got an idea for a song." I don't have my guitar, but we can do it as a rap."

"Go, Nat, go!" said Hector.

"OK," said Nat. "You all can clap to the rap."

"Here we are, on the beach at night,
Looking at the stars, what a wonderful sight!
Sitting with my girl, it just feels so right,
Looking at her eyes that are shining in the moonlight.

There goes Jupiter, there goes Mars,
See the Big Dipper made of seven stars,
Stars held together by the force of gravitation,
Connect the dots, and you get a constellation.

Stars look very tiny, but're really so much bigger,
They are larger than the earth and the planets put together,
Stars are like the sun, but are far away, so they say,
Their light takes years to reach us — they are light years away.

Sun, earth, moon, and stars, and everything we see,
How it all began is a very great mystery.
Science says it started with a Big Bang made of light,
I don't care, as long as I'm here with Kate on the beach at night.

"Nat, that was great," said Kate, giving him a quick kiss. "But I'm not a polar bear. It's chilly on the beach at night. Let's go home."

Comprehension Questions for story #1: *On the Beach at Night*

1. Who is Hector's girlfriend?

2. Who is Kate's boyfriend?

3. About how far is the sun from the earth?

4. How far is the moon from the earth?

5. How many could fit in a straight line across the diameter of the sun?

6. If the sun is so big, why does it look the size of a basketball?

7. Which is the biggest — the earth, the moon, or the sun?

8. Which is the smallest — the earth, moon, or sun?

9. What happens during a solar eclipse? Draw a diagram.

10. What happens during a lunar eclipse? Draw a diagram.

11. The sun is just an average sized _____.

12. A light year is a measure of (a) time (b) size (c) distance

13. Define a light year.

14. What does the Big Bang Theory say?

15. What is the difference between a planet and a star?

16. Hector and Nat began snapping at each other. Who do you think started? Why? Which snap do you like the best?

17. Write the contractions for do not, that is, you are, we are, you have, I will.

WORD LIST #2 (contractions, -tion, per-)

	A	B	C
1	he's = he is	real	sub tract
2	she's = she is	real ly	sub trac tion
3	isn't = is not	real ize	con trac tions
4	we've = we have	real iz a tion	per fect
5	I've = I have	ac tion	per fec tion
6	you'd = you had	mo tion	per spire
7	gas	ro ta tion	per spi ra tion
8		in for ma tion	va por
9		rep u ta tion	e vap or ate
10		sit u a tion	e vap or ates
11		con ver sa tion	e vap or a tion
12		in sin u a tion	re frig er a tion
13		re la tion ship	ab sorb
			ab sorp tion

For Reading Only

sweat
sweet
sweating
scenery
liquid
damaged

Story #2 **(contractions, -tion, per-)**
Concepts: Molecules in solids, liquids and gases; heat, melting, freezing.

Ugly Snaps

"Hector! Get over here right now!" shouted Ann.

"What's up?" Hector asked.

"We've had a relationship for a long time, now. Isn't that right?" Ann asked.

"Yeah. You're my girl," answered Hector.

"Then why is it that whenever a pretty girl walks by you eye them up and down?"

"What are you saying?" asked Hector. "I'm not allowed to look at another girl?"

"What's the matter, I'm not good enough for you?"

"I can't believe we're having this conversation!" said Hector. "Don't you realize that you're the only girl I really care about? We've been together through hard times, and we've always stuck by each other. I've come to the realization that you're the only girl for me. You and I are perfect for each other. So don't get mad if I like to watch girls in motion. I'm only looking at the scenery."

"Well, some of the girls you've been looking at don't have a good reputation. I don't like to be put in a situation where I have to worry about you leaving me for some tramp."

"Ann, you have a real good imagination. Am I the kind of guy who plays the rotation game — one girlfriend this week and another one next week? You're the only girlfriend I've ever had. I don't like your insinuation. Are you accusing me of looking for another girlfriend?"

Just then Flame walked by. She had been jogging, and perspiration was dripping down her face and back. Flame was wearing shorts and a tight tank top that was wet from the absorption of sweat. Hector eyed her up and down.

"There you go again, Hector!" said Ann. "Your eyeballs looks like they're ready to pop out of your head looking at that ugly tramp. You look like you're ready for some action."

"Who are you calling a tramp, girl?" asked Flame in an angry tone. "For your information, I've had the same boyfriend for a whole month!"

"Wow! A whole month!" said Ann. "You'd better watch out, or you'll lose the title of Super Slut."

"You'd better watch out before I slap you upside your head!" said Flame. "The only boyfriend you've ever had is Hector. What's the matter, are you afraid you're too ugly for anybody else?"

"Who are you calling ugly?" asked Ann.

"You!" said Flame. "You're so ugly, you won first prize in the Miss Ugly America contest."

"You're so ugly," answered Ann, "they use your face to make Halloween masks."

"You're so ugly, your only boyfriend is ugly Hector," Flame said with a laugh.

"Your false eyebrows must have damaged your vision," Ann said. "Hector is cute. He's better looking than all the dogs you go out with. I heard you made an R-rated video with them, too scary to be viewed by anyone under 17."

"That's dumb," said Flame.

"Not as dumb as you are," said Ann. "I heard you can't do first grade subtraction. If Flame's head weighs one pound, how much will her head weigh if you subtract the weight of her brain? Duhhh! ... Still one pound."

Just then Nat walked by. Nat was Hector's best friend, even though they liked to snap on each other.

"You guys snapping at each other again?" he asked. "You'd better cool it. Snapping can lead to fights."

"Flame is too hot to get cool," said Hector.

Ann looked hard at Hector and said, "What do you mean by Flame is too hot!!"

"I mean...hot, like...in sweating," Hector said. "Look at all her perspiration. She's hot from running. How can she get cool with all that sweat?"

"For your information, Hector," Nat interrupted, "people perspire in order to get *cool*"

"What, are you nuts?" Hector said. "Whenever I sweat, I get *hot*."

"You've got that backwards, Hector," said Nat. "When you get too hot, you begin to sweat."

"So?"

"So when your sweat dries off you get cool."

"You mean to say I sweat in order to get cool?" asked Ann.

"That's right," said Nat. "Have you ever been to the beach?"

"That's a dumb question," said Ann. "We were just there a few days ago."

"And she looked great in her bathing suit!" added Hector. "She is perfection in a swim suit!"

"Oh, you're so sweet," Ann said turning red.

"I know she's cute in a suit," said Nat. "but when you get out of the water and the wind blows, how do you feel?"

"Cool," said Ann. "The wind on my wet back makes me cold."

"As the water evaporates from your skin, your body cools," said Nat.

"What does evaporate mean?" asked Hector.

"Don't you know?" said Ann. "Evaporation is when water goes up into the air."

"Yes," said Nat. "During evaporation, water changes from a liquid to a gas. The water in your sweat changes from liquid water to a gas called water vapor."

"I thought that when your sweat dries up, the water goes back into your skin," said Hector.

"No, no," said Nat. "The water changes into a gas and goes into the air. The evaporation of water from your skin makes your body feel cool. As the water in perspiration dries up, your body cools off."

"Cool," said Ann.

"Not as cool as you look in a two piece bathing suit," Hector said with a grin.

"Perspiration is made of water and salt," Nat added. "When the water evaporates, the salt stays on your skin. After a while, the body salts begin to smell. That's why you have to shower after you perspire."

"That's why Flame is beginning to stink right now," Ann said with a grin.

"Wipe that grin off your ugly face," said Flame. "You don't have to perspire to stink, Ann. You stink all the time."

Just then, Flame's latest boyfriend, Bubba, walked up.

"Hey Baby," Bubba said to Flame, "you look hot in your shorts and tank top."

"Oh, Bubba," said Flame, "you're so sweet."

Looking at the others, Bubba said, "What's up?"

"Just trying to keep things cool around here," said Nat.

"OK, just keep away from my girl!" Bubba said.

"No sweat," said Nat.

As Bubba walked away with Flame, Flame looked back hard at Ann and said, "This is not over, girl!"

Comprehension Questions for Story #2: *Ugly Snaps*

1. Why was Ann upset at Hector?

2. What is another word for sweat?

3. Why do people perspire?

4. What is evaporation?

5. What is absorption?

6. What is water called when it is a gas?

7. Which ugly snap did you like the best?

8. Write the contractions for: <u>is not</u>, <u>she is</u>, <u>they are</u>, <u>we have</u>, <u>you had</u>

9. Why does Flame say at the end, "This is not over, girl"?

WORD LIST # 3 (contractions, -tion, hu = /yu/)

	A	B	C
1	it's = it is	hu man	cau tion
2	didn't = did not	hu mid	con den sa tion
3	doesn't = does not	hu mid it y	re frig er a tion
4	let's =l et us	hu mor	dis tinc tion
5	shouldn't = should not	sol id	con front
6	where's = where is	va por	con fron ta tion
7		mat ter	ex act ly

For Reading Only

definite
opposite

Story # **3** (contractions, -tion, hu = /yu/; solids, liquids, and gases; condensation, humidity.)

Lips of Honey

Ann, Hector, and Nat watched Flame and Bubba walk away.

"What did she mean by 'This is not over girl'?" asked Nat.

"She thinks she's tough because she has big Bubba to protect her," said Hector.

"I don't care," said Ann. "They don't scare me."

Nat began to perspire.

"Are you sweating because you're scared?" asked Hector.

"I'm sweating because it's hot and humid, and I'm thirsty," Nat answered. "Let's go to the food truck and get some sodas."

Nat and Ann each bought a can of ice-cold cola, but Hector didn't have any money.

"Can I have a sip?" Hector asked Ann.

Ann took a few quick gulps, and handed the can of soda to Hector, who wiped the top of the can with his shirt.

"Why are you wiping the can?" asked Ann.

"Germs," said Hector.

"You're not afraid of my germs when you kiss me," said Ann, "and do you really think your dirty shirt is cleaner than my lips?"

"Ann, your lips are sweet like honey."

"That's right," Said Nat. "Germs don't grow on honey. Did you ever notice that honey doesn't need refrigeration? Honey can sit on the shelf for months without getting spoiled. So Hector is saying that your lips are like honey and don't carry germs."

"Exactly," Hector said with a grin, "that was what I was saying. You have honey lips — a bit sticky, but sweet."

"You better shut your mouth before I give you a fat lip," said Ann. "The heat and humidity must be getting to your head."

"Sorry, Ann," Hector replied. "Where's your sense of humor?" Hector took a long sip of the ice-cold can of soda. The can was wet on the outside.

"Hey," said Hector, "the can is sweating, or leaking or something."

"That's silly," said Nat. "Cans don't perspire, and the can is not leaking. There is only water on the outside, not soda."

"So where does the water on the can come from?" asked Hector.

"From the air," Nat replied.

Hector put the cold wet can against his forehead, and said, "Ah, that feels cool."

"Give me back my soda," said Ann. "You're making it hot!"

"Here, Ann, but I don't get it," Hector said. "If the soda is on the inside, why is the can wet on the outside?"

"Yeah," said Ann. "If I fill a glass with ice, after a while, the glass gets wet on the outside."

"Let Nat the science cat explain," said Nat with a smile. "On a humid day, there is a lot of water in the air."

"I don't see any water in the air," said Hector. "It's not raining."

"Not liquid water," said Nat. "Water vapor — a gas. You can't see water vapor because it is a gas. On a humid day, like today, there is a lot of water vapor in the air."

"So, how does that make the outside of a cold can get wet?" asked Hector.

"When the water vapor in the air hits something cold, the water vapor changes to liquid water," said Nat.

"So that's what happens to a glass of ice water!" said Ann. "When the water vapor in the air hits the cold glass, the gas changes into a liquid."

"That's right!" said Nat. "It's called condensation. It's is the opposite of evaporation. Condensation is when a gas changes into a liquid. Evaporation is when a liquid changes into a gas."

Liquid ——heat / Evaporation——▶ Gas

Gas ——cool / Condensation——▶ Liquid

"So, when I come out of the water after a swim, the water on my skin evaporates and goes into the air," said Ann.

"That's right — evaporation."

"And as the water evaporates from my skin, my skin gets cool," Ann added. "OK, so what happens when I take a shower, and the bathroom window gets wet and the mirror gets all fogged up?"

"The water from the shower evaporates, and fills the bathroom with water vapor — water in the form of a gas," said Nat. "When the water vapor hits the cold glass, it changes into a film of liquid water. So liquid water in the shower first evaporates into a gas. Then the gas changes back to a liquid when it hits something cooler, like the window or the mirror."

"Let's go check it out, Ann," Hector said with a grin. "You and I can take a shower together and see if the window gets wet."

"You really *do* want a fat lip," said Ann.

"If you do hit me in the lip, one kiss from your your lips of honey will make it all better," kidded Hector. "If not, I can always get a kiss from Flame."

"One word of caution," said Ann. "You can pass out if you get too close to Flame's smelly arm pit. When the water in her perspiration evaporates, you'll need a gas mask."

"Flame is a human being," said Nat. "We shouldn't be snapping on her behind her back."

"OK," said Ann, "I'll save my snaps when I confront her in person."

"It would be better to avoid a confrontation," said Nat. "We don't need Bubba getting mad at us, too."

"Bubba is full of hot air," said Hector.

"And air is a gas," said Nat.

"OK," said Hector. "I don't get this gas and liquid thing. Isn't ice solid water?"

"That's right," said Ann. "Water can be a solid, too."

"What's the difference between a solid, liquid, and a gas?" asked Hector.

"Everything that has weight or takes up space is called *matter*," said Nat. A chair is is made of matter; water is made of matter; air in a balloon is made of matter. There are three forms of matter: solids, liquids and gases. It's important to understand the distinction between the three. Rocks, pencils, and ice are solids. Solids keep their shape."

"Hector's head is hard as a rock, so it must be solid," kidded Ann.

"Flame must be solid too, because she sure has a definite shape," said Hector.

"If I smack you on your lip you will get to see a liquid — a red liquid," Ann replied.

"That's right, Ann!" said Nat. "Blood is a liquid. Water and milk are liquids, too. Liquids can change their shape. You can pour water into a tall glass or into a flat pan, and the water will take the shape of the container. Liquids do not have a definite shape, but they do have a definite volume — they take up a definite amount of space."

"And what about a gas?" asked Hector.

"A gas does not have a shape," said Nat. "A gas spreads out and fills its container. If you boil water, the liquid water changes into a gas, and the gas spreads out into the room. Gases do not have a definite shape or a definite volume."

"Yeah," said Hector. "When my mom is boiling water, the water vapor goes into the air. If it's cold outside, the windows get all fogged up. That must be due to condensation. When the water vapor hits the cold glass, the gas changes into a liquid."

"Hey, Hector," Ann said with a grin, "you're not as dumb as you look."

"It must be because I just drank soda from a can that touched your lips," Hector said to Ann. "Your honey lips must be making me smart."

Comprehension Questions

1. Why did Hector wipe off the top of the soda can?

2. What is in the air on a humid day?

3. In condensation, a _____ changes into a _____.

4. Why is evaporation the opposite of condensation?

5. Next to each phrase, write solid, liquid or gas:
      a. ice _____
      b. air _____
      c. juice _____
      d. keeps its shape _____
      e. has no shape, spreads out and fills any container _____
      f. takes the shape of the container _____
      g. does **not** have a definite shape or a definite volume _____
      h. has a definite shape and a definite volume _____
      i. does not have a definite shape, but does have a definite volume _____

6. What happens when water vapor hits a cold window?
   The water vapor changes into a _____ .

7. When there are a lot of people in a car during the winter, why do the inside windows get fogged up?

WORD LIST #4 (-ule, -ful, -ous, -ious)
Concepts: Molecules in solids, liquids and gases; heat, melting, freezing

	A	B	C
1	mule	full	joy ous
2	rule	bull	rid ic u lous
3	ru ler	aw ful	fam ous
4	tu lip	bash ful	nerv ous
5	tru ly	beau ti ful	e nor mous
6	un ru ly	faith ful	fab u lous
7	cap sule	un faith ful	fu ri ous
8	cap sules	cal cu late	cu ri ous
9	rid i cule	de liv er	hi lar i ous
10	mol e cule	prop er ty	se ri ous
11	mol e cules	ex pla na tion	ob vi ous
12	gran ule	reg u lar	com plete ly
13	min us cule	mi cro scope	re spon si bil i ty
	won't = will not		

For Reading Only

ambulance

peculiar

jealous

anxious

schedule

pharmacy

medicine

excitement

shelves

artificial

either

Story #4 (-ule, -ful, -ous, -ious) © **Daniel Langer**
Concepts: Molecules in solids, liquids and gases; heat, melting, freezing.

Hector Gets a Job

A few days later, Nat was at home watching TV. The doorbell rang, and Nat got up and opened the door.

"Hey, Hector, come on in. What's up?"

"I just got a summer job at the pharmacy!" Hector said with excitement. "I'll be working in Mr. Kooper's drug store!"

"Wow!" said Nat. "You have a regular summer job! That's fabulous!"

"I have to put medicine on the shelves," said Hector.

"I'm curious, what else will you be doing there?"

"I also have to deliver medicine to sick people,"

"That's a serious job. It's an enormous responsibility, but it sounds like fun. You get to go outside, and you get paid for it. When do you start?"

"Tomorrow morning."

"Does that mean we won't be able to hang out together anymore?"

"As a rule, I'll be working only mornings during the summer. I can still get together with everyone in the afternoon and evening."

"That is a great schedule," said Nat. "You get to make money and you don't miss out on having fun with your friends. You must be full of joy!"

"I don't feel joyous," said Hector. "I feel nervous and anxious. People are going to come into the store and ask me questions, and I won't know the answer. I don't know a thing about health and science. I don't even know the difference between a capsule and a tablet."

"Don't feel nervous," said Nat. "No need to feel anxious. I'm Nat the famous science cat. You can ask me anything. A capsule has tiny granules of medicine packed inside."

"I don't understand. What's a granule?"

"Something like grains of salt or sugar," said Nat. "Would you like a soda?"

"Sure, with some ice," said Hector. "Make sure it has real sugar in it. I don't like diet soda."

"Good choice. Artificial sugar is worse than real sugar, but real sugar is not good for you, either." Nat poured some cola in a glass of ice and gave it to Hector.

"By the way," Hector asked. "Why can't you see the granules of sugar in soda?"

"When sugar dissolves in water, the bits of sugar become too minuscule to see," Nat answered.

"Minuscule?"

"Yeah, minuscule, very, very tiny.

"Oh, minuscule," Hector said. "Tiny like the size of Bubba's brain."

"You'd better not let Bubba hear you ridicule him like that, or he'll sit on you and make you as flat as a ruler. Bubba is enormous. You will feel like a fool who got crushed by a mule."

Hector took a quick gulp of soda, and then he took out an ice cube and rubbed it on his face. The ice began to melt in Hectors hand.

Hector looked at Nat. "OK, science cat, do you remember the other day when we were talking about evaporation and condensation? I understand that evaporation is when a liquid changes into a gas, and that condensation is when a gas changes into a liquid. I know that when you freeze water, the water changes into solid ice, and when the ice melts, it changes back to liquid water. But how does it all work? Why is the ice in my hand melting?"

"It's melting because your hand is warm," said Nat.

"No, duh! Any fool knows that!"

Nat was a bit upset with Hector. "No need to ridicule me, Hector."

"OK, but how does my warm hand change solid ice into liquid water?"

"Let's start from the beginning. "Water is made of tiny water molecules."

"I've heard of molecules," said Hector. "What exactly are they?"

"A molecule is the smallest bit of anything. The smallest amount of water is one molecule of water. The smallest bit of gold is one molecule of gold. The smallest bit of sugar is one molecule of sugar."

"That's easy," said Hector. "Everything is made of tiny molecules."

"They are so minuscule, you can't see them," said Nat, "not even with a microscope."

"What do molecules have to do with solids, liquids, and gasses?" asked Hector.

"In a solid, the molecules are packed tight. The molecules don't move around. That's why solids keep their shape."

"OK," said Hector, "an ice cube or an iron nail keeps its shape because each is a solid. In a solid, the molecules are packed tight and don't move around. So how does heat make an ice cube melt?"

"Heat makes molecules move faster," Nat replied. "If you heat an ice cube, the water molecules in the ice start moving around. When that happens, the molecules are no longer packed together, and the ice begins to melt."

"So my warm hand is making the ice cube melt," said Hector. "Heat can change solid water into liquid water."

"That's right," said Nat. "In a liquid, the molecules move around."

"So that's why liquids can change their shape!" said Hector. "The molecules move around! When you pour water from a pitcher into a glass, the molecules move around and take the shape of the glass."

"You've got it," said Nat.

"Cool," said Hector. "So when you freeze a liquid, the molecules stop moving around. It's like if you tell everyone to freeze, you want them to stop moving. Can heat melt a solid iron nail?"

"It takes a lot of heat to make the molecules in an iron nail move around," said Nat, "but with enough heat, even iron can melt."

By now, the ice cube in Hector's hand had melted completely. Hector walked over to the window because he was still a little hot. Flame was crossing the street.

"There goes Flame," Hector said, "the girl with the definite shape, and don't tell Ann I said that!"

"I'm cool," said Nat. "I'm not going to tell Ann about how your eyes pop out of your head every time Flame walks by."

"If you do," joked Nat, "I'll pop you in the head."

Hector's hand was dry now. The melted ice had evaporated.

"One more question," Hector said. "My hand was wet from the melted ice. Now it's dry. What made the water evaporate? What makes a liquid change into a gas?"

"Let me ask *you* a question," said Nat. "If you heat water in a pot, what happens to the speed of the molecules?"

"Heat makes molecules move faster," said Hector.

"That's right!" said Nat. "So the hotter it gets the faster the water molecules move around. As the water heats up, the water molecules move faster and faster. Soon, the molecules begin to fly off into the air. When that happens, the liquid water changes into a gas."

"Heat makes water evaporate," said Hector. "But if I spill water on the table, the water evaporates without heating it."

"That's true," said Nat. "The molecules in liquid water are moving around all the time. Every once in a while, some of them fly off into the air. Eventually, they all fly up into the air, and all the water evaporates."

"So the table doesn't absorb the water," Hector said. "The water molecules fly up into the air. Heat makes water evaporate faster. If I put a wet towel in the sun, it will dry off faster."

"You've got it!" said Nat. "The heat from the sun makes the water molecules move faster, so the water evaporates more quickly."

Just then, the doorbell rang. Nat opened the door. It was Ann and Kate.

"Come on in," said Nat. "You girls look fabulous!"

"Nat, stop looking at my girl!" said Hector.

"But they are both truly beautiful," Nat replied. "I'm not bashful. If I see a truly beautiful girl, I am not afraid to say so."

"Ann is *my* girl," said Hector. "I don't want you making a pass at her. You look at her again, and you're going to need an ambulance!"

"Hector," said Ann, "Your behavior is awful. What you are saying is ridiculous! I am not your property! You are not my ruler! I have always been faithful to you. I cannot calculate how many times boys have wanted to go out with me, but I turned them down for *you*. If you keep treating me like you own me, you can find a new girlfriend!"

"That's bull!" said Hector. "When did another boy ever ask you out?"

"Nat did once,"said Ann. "He even asked me to kiss him."

"Nat!" said Kate. "Is that true? Have you been unfaithful to me?"

"Well," said Nat scratching his head, "that was a long time ago — before I met you."

"That's bull," said Hector. "You've always been after Ann."

"No, I have not," said Nat. "I like Kate. She is the girl for me. I want to be with her for the rest of my life. So cool it! We are all friends. No need to act like a bunch of unruly fools."

"It's not his fault," said Ann, "Hector acts like a fool because he looks like a mule."

"That must be why I love, you," said Hector. "You know how much a mule loves to eat flowers. You are as beautiful as a tulip, and this mule wants to kiss your two lips."

"Very good, Hector," said Ann. "Tulips...two lips. I didn't know you could calculate all the way up to the number *two*."

"Ann, I don't like it when you ridicule me," said Hector. "I was acting like a jealous fool, but I don't look like a mule. Anyway, I'm nervous about my new job. That's why I'm acting so strange. I didn't even know the difference between condensation and evaporation."

"You have been acting peculiar," said Ann. "If you keep having these jealous fits, our relationship will evaporate into thin air. In order to have a solid relationship, you've got to trust me."

"Yes, a solid relationship," said Hector. "In a solid, molecules don't move around. Solids have a definite shape and a definite volume. Our relationship should not change just because Nat said you are beautiful."

"Sorry to interrupt," said Kate, "but we came here to give Hector a message."

"Oh yes," said Ann. "Mr. Kooper wants you to come to the pharmacy right now. You have to deliver some medicine to someone who needs it right away!"

Comprehensions Questions

1. Give two examples of something found in the kitchen that is made of tiny granules.

2. What does the word minuscule mean?

3. What is a molecule?

4. What does heat do to the speed of molecules?

For the questions 5—10, fill in the word solid, liquid or gas—

5. Molecules don't move around in a _____.

6. Heat makes the molecules in an ice cube start to move. When the molecules in ice start moving, the ice becomes a _____.

7. Molecules move around in a _____.

8. Molecules move very fast and fly around in a _____.

9. Because their molecules can move around, a _____ takes the shape of its container.

10. Which has a definite shape and definite volume: a solid, a liquid, or a gas? _____.

11. What happens to water when it is heated in a pot? Include the movement of the water molecules in your explanation.

12. If water is spilled on a table, it can dry up by itself. Where did the water _molecules_ go?

13. Why was Hector angry at Nat?

14. Why was Ann upset with Hector?

15. What is Hector's new job? What does he have to do at this job?

16. Why is Hector anxious about his new job?

WORD LIST #5 (c=k; c=s: ci, ce, cy) © Daniel Langer

	A	B	C
1	cell	ci ty	cy cle
2	cent	ci der	bi cy cle
3	cen ter	cir cus	tri cy cle
4	de cent	de cide	re cy cle
5	ice	ci gar	mo tor cy cle
6	con cert	cir cle	fan cy
7	chan ces	cir cu lar	spice
8	can cer	cir cu la tion	spi cy
9	space	cir cu la tor y	mer cy
10	sub stance	cal ci um	lu na cy
11	cop y	ex cite ment	pri va cy
12	wel come	cell mem brane	fre quen cy
13	care ful	ac ci dent	fre quent ly
14	to bac co	nu cle us	cy to plasm
15	con trols	couch	en cy clo pe di a
16	con fused	counter	mic ro scope
17	con tact	cus tom ers	a part ment
18	ac tiv it y	des troy	sys tem

For Reading Only

decision	juice
cigarette	terrace
certain	muscle
uncertain	disease
cell division	coughing

Story #5 (c=k; c=s: ci, ce, cy) © Daniel Langer
Concepts: Cells: nucleus, cytoplasm, cell membrane; concept of cell division; cigarettes and cancer; sun block.

Hector Goes to Flame's Apartment

Mr. Kooper was behind the counter when Hector walked into the pharmacy.

"Welcome, Hector," Mr. Kooper said. "I'm glad you were able to come to work on such short notice. I usually don't send out deliveries at night, but one of my customers ran out of medicine, and he needs to have it tonight. Take this to Mr. Sam Jones at 125 Godwin Terrace, apartment 3A."

"I think I know a Jones living on Godwin Terrace," Hector said. "Does Mr. Jones have a daughter, Flame Jones?"

"I don't know her by that name, but he does have a daughter, a very pretty girl. She comes by frequently to pick up her father's medicine."

"What's wrong with her father?" Hector asked.

"He has cancer," Mr. Kooper replied. "He started smoking cigarettes as a teenager. Now he is very sick and may die."

"Smoking cigarettes gave him cancer?"

"Yes. If you smoke, all that smoke gets trapped in your lungs. Many people get cancer, heart disease, or lung disease from smoking cigarettes."

"What about cigars?"

"Cigars can give you cancer of the mouth or throat. People who get throat cancer may have to have their voice boxes taken out. Then they can't talk."

"I think I'll stay away from tobacco, Mr. Kooper."

"That's a smart decision, Hector."

"My girlfriend, Ann, says she will never kiss a guy that smells from cigarettes."

"That's right. Cigarettes makes your breath and clothing stink, and it makes your teeth turn yellow."

"That's gross. What are the chances of getting cancer from smoking? If I smoke just one cigarette, could I get cancer?"

"The chance of getting cancer depends on the frequency. The more frequently you smoke the greater the chances of getting sick. Even smoking one cigarette a day could give you cancer."

"How do cigarettes give you cancer?"

"Putting that junk into your lungs can change a normal cell into a cancer cell."

"What exactly is a cell, Mr. Kooper?"

"Hector, do you see that house across the street?"

"Yes."

"What is it made of?"

"Bricks."

"Well, just as a house is made of bricks, living things are made of cells. Cells are very small. You can only see them with a microscope."

"You mean cells are tiny like molecules?"

"Molecules are much smaller than cells. Molecules are so small you can't even see them with a microscope. There are millions of water and protein molecules in one cell."

"What do cells look like?"

Mr. Kooper drew a circle with a smaller circle inside.

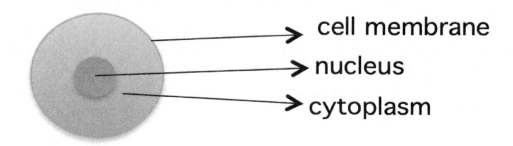

"Cells come in different shapes, depending upon the type of cell. Skin cells are flat. Muscle cells are long and thin. But most cells have three basic parts. They have on outer cover called the cell membrane. They are filled with a jelly-like substance called cytoplasm. Near the center is something that looks like a little round ball called the nucleus. The nucleus controls cell activity, such as cell growth and cell division."

"What is cell division?"

"During cell division, the nucleus makes a copy of itself. Then the cell divides. The cell splits in half and becomes two cells."

"So what is a cancer cell?"

"If you cut your skin, your skin cells next to the cut begin to divide until they fill up the space where the cut was. When the skin cells come in contact with each other, they stop dividing. Cancer cells don't stop dividing. They keep on dividing again and again and again, until they form a lump. Some of these cancer cells may travel to other part of the body and start growing into lumps of cells that shouldn't be there. These cancer cells can destroy parts of your body and kill you."

"Can the sun cause skin cancer?"

"Yes. Too much sun can cause skin cancer. Sun block can help stop your skin cells from changing into cancer cells."

"How do cancer cells spread?"

"Cancer usually begins as a lump of cells. After a while, some cancer cells break off and get carried around by the blood. The blood moves around your body in a circular path, from the heart to the blood vessels and and back to the heart. The movement of blood around the body is called circulation, from the word circle. The heart and all the blood vessels make up the circulatory system."

"Mr. Kooper, you're like a walking encyclopedia. You know everything, but don't I have to make a delivery?"

"Oh yes," said Mr. Kooper. "Here's the medicine for Mr. Jones, and some calcium pills for his wife. Calcium keeps the bones strong. You can get minerals like calcium from milk, cheese, and dark green vegetables, but if you don't eat enough of *that* you can get some of what you need in a pill. You can take the pharmacy bike to make your delivery."

"You have a motorcycle for deliveries?" Hector asked with excitement.

"Not a motorcycle, a tricycle," Mr. Kooper said with a grin.

"A tricycle! I'm not riding a tricycle! I don't want to look like a circus clown!"

"Only kidding, Hector. Take the pharmacy *bicycle*. It's in the back, and be careful riding the bike. I don't want you getting into an accident."

The bicycle had a large basket in front with a metal plate that said *Kooper's Pharmacy.* Hector put the package in the basket and rode to 125 Godwin Terrace. He chained the bicycle to a pole, entered the building, and went up to apartment 3A.

Hector rang the bell. A pretty girl wearing a fancy nightgown answered the door. It was Flame.

"Hector! What are you doing here!" Flame asked with a smile.

"I have a delivery for Mr. Sam Jones from Kooper's Pharmacy."

"Come on in, Hector."

"I just came to make a delivery."

"You can come in for just a second, can't you, Hector?"

"I guess so." Hector said, as he walked into Flame's apartment. Hector thought to himself, "This is lunacy. If Ann finds out I was at Flame's apartment and that she was wearing a nightgown, Ann will kill me!"

"Wait a second, while I put on something decent," Flame said. "Have a seat on the couch." Hector couldn't take his eyes off her as she walked into her bedroom and returned wearing a robe over her fancy nightgown.

"Would you like an ice cold glass of milk or a glass of cider?" Flame asked. "Milk has calcium. It's good for your bones. Cider is made from the juice of apples. Decide — milk or juice?"

"I don't like milk," Hector replied. "I'll take the cider. I could use an ice cold drink to cool me off. Looking at you makes me feel warm all over."

Flame brought Hector a large glass of ice-cold apple cider, and sat down next to Hector on the couch.

"You're kind of cute, Hector" Flame said.

"I thought you like big boys like Bubba," Hector said.

"We're not going steady, or anything," Flame said. "Bubba had great tickets to a concert, so I went out with him. Now he thinks he's my boyfriend. I've had my eye on you for a long time Hector." Flame sat a little closer to Hector.

"I never thought I'd be making a delivery to your house, Flame," Hector said.

"You can call me Samantha. Flame is my nickname. Some boys thought I was hot and spicy like the Spice Girls, so they called me Flame. The name stuck. I don't mind the nickname, but my good friends call me Samantha."

Just then, some loud coughing could be heard in the apartment.

"That's my father," Flame said. "He's very sick. He's going to die."

"Are you certain he's going to die?"

"The doctor said he has less than a year to live. I wish God would have mercy on my father." Flame began to cry, and she put her arms around Hector and cried on his shoulder. Hector patted her on the back to comfort her. He liked the way Flame felt as she rested her head on his shoulder, but he was thinking about Ann. The sound of coughing could be heard again.

"I feel bad about your father," Hector said.

"Sometimes I think life is just one cycle of pain," Flame said, as she dried her eyes with a tissue. I'd better get this medicine you brought to my father."

When she came back, she said, "My mother will be home from work pretty soon. Maybe you'd better go now. My father said to give the delivery boy a fifty cent tip."

"I don't want a tip from you, Samantha. Anyway, you did give me a glass of ice cold cider."

""Could you take the empty glass bottle of cider and put it in the recycle bin on your way out?" Flame asked.

"Sure Samantha, anything you say."

"I like it when you call me Samantha," Flame said. "I hope we can meet again when we can have more privacy."

As Hector walked out the door, Flame smiled and said, "I'll be looking forward to your next delivery."

Hector tossed the cider bottle in the glass recycle bin and ran down the steps. Hector felt confused and uncertain about whether he should decide to see Flame again. He was thinking, "What will Ann think if she finds out I was at Flame's apartment? My father said there are no accidents in this world. There is a reason for everything. Was it an accident that from all the people in the city that needed medicine, I ended up making a delivery to Flame's father?"

Comprehension Questions for *Hector Goes to Flame's Apartment*

1. Smoking cigarettes can give you _____.

2. Can smoking a cigar give you cancer? _____ Where? _____

3. What made Hector decide that he didn't want to smoke?

4. Some houses are made of bricks. Living things are made of _____.

5. Which is much smaller, a cell or a molecule?

6. Name three parts of the cell

7. Which part of the cell controls cell activity?

8. The outer cover of a cell is called the _____ _____.

9. The jelly-like substance that fills the cell is the _____.

10. Why is it bad to sunbathe?

11. How can you protect yourself from the sun?

12. Just before a cell divides, the nucleus makes a _____ of itself.

13. How is a cancer cell different from a normal cell?

14. Why did Hector call Mr. Kooper a walking encyclopedia?

15. The mineral calcium is needed for healthy _____.

16. Do you think Hector was glad he had to make a delivery to Flame's father?

17. What is Flame's real name?

18. What do you think is going to happen between Hector, Flame, and Ann?

WORD LIST 6 (ph, sph, tch, plurals with es)

	A	B	C
1	fa ces	itch	phone
2	clo ses	itch es	pho ny
3	cur ses	inch es	tel e phone
4	cau ses	watch	sax o phone
5	hou ses	witch	meg a phone
6	bus ses	witch es	head phones
7	glas ses	kit chen	pho to
8	kiss es	match	pho to graph
9	ill nes ses	match es	pho tog ra pher
10	or bit	catch	or phan
11	star va tion	scratch	tro phy
12	rev o lu tion	scratch ing	phase
13	wind pipe	scratch es	Phil
14	up hill	stitch es	pho bi a
15	snake	such	sphere
16	snakes	sand wich	at mos sphere
17	liz ards	sand wich es	hem i sphere
18	rep tiles	branche	dol phin
19	croc o diles	branch es	el e phant
20	mam mals	ro tate	am phib i an
21	sal a man ders	ro tates	e soph a gus
22	im ag i nar y	ro ta tion	phar ma cist
23		re volves	phy si cal

For Reading Only

nephew   lifeguard

pollution   cough

axis   coughing

which   coughed

turtles   temperature

emphysema

crescent moon

WORD LIST 6 (ph, sph, tch, plurals with es) © Daniel Langer
Concepts: Amphibians, reptiles, mammals, day, night, month, year, lunar phases, seasons

Photographs on the Beach

Hector was playing his saxophone, when the phone rang.

"Hector!" his mother called from the kitchen. "Telephone! It's for you!"

Hector put down his saxophone, and picked up the cordless telephone. "I've got it, Mom. You can hang up now."

"Hello," Hector said, as he took the phone and walked into his room for some privacy.   "Ann? Hi!

I was playing the sax.

What's up?

Of course I want to see you. I was going to call you later. I had to go to work this morning, but I'm free for the afternoon.

Go to the beach with you, Nat, and Kate? I'd love to. I love the beach in the late afternoon. It's not crowded, and I like to watch the sun set. When?

In an hour?

OK.

No, not that bus stop. It's an uphill walk. I'll meet you guys at the other bus stop.

OK."

It was a long bus ride to Orchard Beach. Ann was listening to her cellphone with her headphones. Kate was looking at her camera. Kate loved taking photographs. She was a very good photographer.

When they got off the bus, they quickly walked to the beach. There was only an hour of daylight left.

"Let me take a photo of you two love birds," Kate said to Ann and Hector.

Hector put his arm around Ann, and Kate took a picture. "Great, the sun lit up your faces, and the water was in the background."

"Look at that sun!" said Ann.

"And look at that sky — clear blue." said Nat. "No pollution in the atmosphere today!"

"Let's go for a swim," said Kate.

They all stripped down to their bathing suits, which they were wearing under their clothing. Hector dived in first, and swam quickly into deep water.

"Hector, you're a good swimmer," Kate said as she slowly swam out to Hector.

"I won a trophy for swimming once," Hector said.

"I wish there were dolphins in this water," Kate said as Ann caught up to them "I'd love to take a photograph of one."

"Watch this! I'm a dolphin!" Hector said as he dived under Ann's legs.

"Hey, you all!" called Nat, who was standing in water up to his waist. "You guys are out too deep for me."

"Let's play leapfrog in the shallow water," said Kate. Nat was afraid of the deep water, and she didn't want to leave him all alone.

Kate bent down, and Nat jumped over her. "You did that just like a frog," Hector said.

"Are you calling me an amphibian?" Nat yelled at Hector.

"A what?" Hector asked.

"An amphibian — an animal that can live on both land and in water," Nat replied.

"Like a turtle?" asked Ann.

"No, like a frog," replied Nat. "A turtle is a reptile, not an amphibian."

"But a turtle can live on both land and in water, so what's the difference between an amphibian and a reptile?" Ann asked.

"Amphibians, such as frogs and salamanders, have smooth skin and they lay their eggs in water. Reptiles, like turtles, snakes, lizards, and crocodiles, have scales on their skin, and they always lay their eggs on land. Except for snakes, reptiles alao have claws; amphibians do not."

"Then Ann must be an amphibian," Hector joked while rubbing his hand on her arm. "She has smooth skin."

"But don't let me scratch you," Ann joked. "I have claws like a reptile."

Ann tried to jump over Hector, but landed on his head.

"We're playing leapfrog, not leap elephant," said Hector.

Ann slapped Hector in the face.

"Hey, you don't have to get physical," Hector said. "I was only joking."

"You're such a phony," said Ann. "You meant it. First you call me an amphibian, then you call me an elephant!"

"I was only kidding around," Hector said while rubbing his face.

Ann began to cry, "I don't like that kind of kidding around," she said.

"I'm sorry," said Hector. "But you didn't have to slap me in the face."

"I'm sorry, too" said Ann. "Let me kiss it." Ann put her arms around Hector and gave him a kiss on his face.

"Now that's the kind of physical I like," said Hector.

Just then Kate screamed. "Snakes! Snakes are in the water!' Kate jumped on Nat and began to scream and shake all over, because she thought she saw a snake"

Those aren't snakes," said Ann picking up a thin tree branch. "Look, it's only some tree branches floating in the water."

Kate was still hugging Nat tightly and shaking all over. "I'm really scared of snakes."

"Don't be scared," said Nat. "There aren't any snakes in the water — only some tree branches that must have fallen from a tree during a storm."

Kate began to relax.

"I think you have a phobia," said Ann.

"What's a phobia?" asked Hector.

"A phobia is a very strong fear of something," said Ann. "Kate seems to have a snake phobia."

"Well, I have a starvation phobia," kidded Hector. "If I don't eat soon, I'm afraid I might die. Let's get out of the water and eat our sandwiches."

They all ran out of the water and began drying themselves with towels.

"I forgot my towel," said Ann. "I'm freezing."

"Here, Ann," said Hector. "Use my towel. You could catch a cold."

"Why am I so cold?" asked Ann. "I was warmer in the water."

"I remember," said Hector. "When you came out of the water, the water on your skin began evaporating. When water evaporates from your skin, it makes you feel cool."

"That's right," said Kate. "That's why we sweat when we're hot. When the water in sweat evaporates, the skin cools off."

"I'm glad you all remember that, but I'm still freezing!" said Ann.

Hector put his arms around Ann. "Thank you," Hector. "Your warm arms make me feel much better."

"My back itches," said Hector. "Could you scratch the itch on my back? ... Not too hard! I like soft scratches on my back."

Ann began scratching Hector's back.

"Not there — a few inches higher," Hector said. " Oh, that's it - NOT SO HARD!!! Your nails are too sharp! Don't cut me with those sharp nails! I thought only witches had nails like that! If you scratch me that hard with those nails, I'll have to get stitches! "

"Go scratch your own back," said Ann. "I don't like getting orders."

"Time to eat!" said Kate. "I brought some sandwiches for everyone."

Everyone began to eat, but Ann was still upset with Hector. Ann took a bite of her sandwich, and started to yell at Hector. Then she began to choke on her food. She couldn't breathe."

Hector slapped her on her back, but it didn't help. Ann was still choking. Nat ran quickly to Ann. He stood behind her, and put his arms around her waist, made a fist, and pushed hard against her belly. Ann coughed up the food that had been stuck in her windpipe.

"What happened?" asked Kate.

"Normally, when we swallow, food goes down our esophagus," said Nat.

"Esophagus?"

"The esophagus is the food pipe. The esophagus is a muscular tube that connects the mouth to the stomach. In front the esophagus is another pipe, called the windpipe. When we breathe, air goes down the windpipe into our lungs. Ann was trying to talk and swallow at the same time, so the food went down the wrong pipe. The food went into her windpipe, instead of her esophagus. So she began to choke. When I pressed hard on her upper belly, I forced air from her lungs out of her windpipe. The food that was stuck in her windpipe popped out."

"You saved my life, Nat!" Ann said after she stopped coughing. Ann gave Nat a kiss on his cheek. "Thank you."

"And I saved you from freezing," said Hector. "You didn't give *me* a kiss!"

"I gave you a kiss after I slapped your face," said Ann. "Do you want another slap? You said I have nails like a witch and I don't think you liked kisses from witches."

"That depends upon which witch it is," Hector replied. "You are my favorite witch."

"Watch it, Hector!"

"OK, guys," said Kate. "Stop fighting. Look at that sunset in the western sky! It's so beautiful! I wish we could come here early in the morning to see the sun rise in the east over the water."

"Where does the sun go after it sets?" asked Ann. "How do we get day and night?"

"The earth is a sphere, like a large ball that spins around itself once each day," said Nat. "A day is the amount of time it takes the earth to make one spin, one rotation, around its own axis."

"What's the earth's axis?" asked Ann.

"The earth's axis is an imaginary line drawn from the North Pole to the South Pole, right through the center of the earth," said Nat. "The earth rotates around its axis like a spinning top. Each rotation takes a day. When we are facing the sun, it is daylight. When we rotate away from the sun, it's nighttime."

"Look at the moon," said Kate. "Isn't the moon beautiful? When we were here last week, it was a full moon. Now it's a half moon. Next week we will see a crescent moon — the phase of the moon that looks like a banana."

"It takes the moon about a month to go through all of its phases," said Nat. "During that time, the moon makes one trip around the earth."

"That must be why we call it a *month* — after the word *moon*!" said Ann.

"That's right," said Nat. "It takes about a month for the moon to make one revolution around the earth. The path that the moon takes as it revolves around the earth is called the moon's orbit around the earth." Let me draw a picture in the sand.

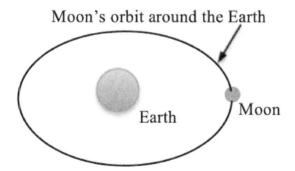
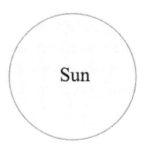

"So what makes a year?" Ann asked.

"A year is the amount of time it takes the earth to go around the sun. The path the earth takes while it revolves all around the sun is the earth's orbit. Every planet has its own orbit around the sun."

Nat drew this picture:

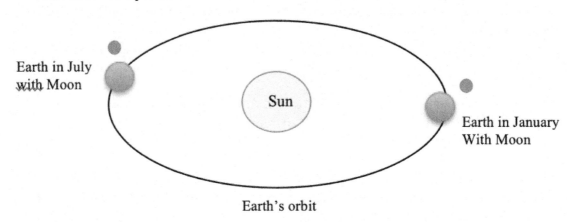

Earth's orbit

"You mean it takes the earth 365 days to make one revolution around the sun?" asked Hector.

"365 1/4 days, to be exact," Nat answered. "As the earth makes one revolution around the sun in a year, the earth rotates 365 1/4 times."

"So how do we get seasons?" asked Kate. "Why is it warm in the summer and cold in winter?"

"I know why," said Hector. "I feel warmer in the summer because Ann gives me more hugs in the summer than she does in the winter."

"That's silly," said Ann. "I think I know why. Doesn't it have to do with the earth's tilt?"

"Yes!" said Nat. "The equator is an imaginary line drawn around the middle of the earth. If we split a globe at the equator, the top part is the Northern Hemisphere, and the bottom part is the Southern Hemisphere."

"I get it," said Kate. "A sphere is a ball, and a hemisphere is half a ball, but what does that have to do with the earth's tilt?"

"When it is summer in the Northern Hemisphere, it is winter in the Southern Hemisphere," said Nat. "In July, the Northern Hemisphere is tilted *towards* the sun. The sun is higher in the sky, and the days are long and the nights short. The long hours of daylight and the high sun makes it warmer in summer. However, the Southern Hemisphere has winter in July, because it is tilted *away* from the sun. In July, the Southern Hemisphere has short days and long nights, and the sun is low in the sky. The short hours of daylight, long nights, and low angle of the sun makes it cold in winter."

"We live in the Northern Hemisphere," said Kate. "In July, our hemisphere is tilted towards the sun, and we have summer. Six months later, in January, we have made a half revolution to the other side of the sun. Our Northern Hemisphere is tilted away from the sun, and we have winter"

"You've got the idea," said Nat. "Do you see the sun setting over there? It is 93,000,000 miles away from us. Think about this. In six months, we will all be on the other side of the sun, and it will be winter here in the Northern Hemisphere."

They sat on the sand eating their sandwiches, until it began to get dark.

"Hey look," said Hector. "The stars are coming out."

Kate reached into her bag and took out her eyeglasses. "I can see the stars better with my glasses on."

"I didn't know you wore glasses," said Ann.

"You look cute in them," said Nat.

"I just got them," Kate said. "I can see much better with them. Now I can see the stars. I can see the leaves on the trees, and the houses in the distance. But I can't see them clearly without my glasses."

"You should wear them all the time," said Ann. "You don't want to miss anything because you can't see."

"But I'm afraid boys won't like me if I wear eyeglasses."

"I like you," said Nat. "You are beautiful, with glasses or without glasses."

"Nat, you're so sweet," said Kate.

"But you do look cute with glasses," Nat said. "You are the most beautiful girl I ever saw."

"That is why I love you," said Kate. "When you say I look cute, you are not being a phony. You always mean what you say." Kate gave Nat a quick kiss on the lips.

Just then, two dogs ran across the beach. They jumped into the water, and then ran back to the sand.

Kate grabbed her camera and took some photographs of the dogs.

"Hey, dogs can swim in water and walk on land," said Hector. "Amphibians lay their eggs in water, and reptiles lay their eggs on land. So what is dog — an amphibian or a reptile?"

"Dogs don't lay eggs, silly," said Kate. "Dogs are mammals. Mammals have hair or fur, and female mammals give milk to their young."

"Here girl, here girl" shouted Kate. The dogs ran over to Kate, and Kate began to pet them. "Aren't these dogs nice looking bitches."

"Watch your language, Kate," said Nat. "I don't like anyone who curses."

"Bitch isn't a curse," said Kate. "A bitch is a female dog."

"Oh, like Flame," said Ann.

"I guess it depends upon how you use the word," said Kate. "No one should use that word when talking about a person. We are human beings, not dogs."

Just then, Phil the lifeguard, walked by. "Do you have any matches?" he asked. "I need a match to light my cigarette."

"We don't smoke!" shouted Nat. "Lifeguards shouldn't be smoking. You can get out of breath if you have to save someone. Smoking causes all kinds of illnesses, like cancer and emphysema. People with emphysema can't breathe. They feel like they are drowning, and no lifeguard can save them."

"Nobody asked your advice, punk," said Phil. "Get off the beach! The beach is closing."

Phil picked up his megaphone, and called out, "Everyone off the beach! The beach closes in ten minutes! Last busses from Orchard Beach leave in fifteen minutes!"

"We'd better hurry," said Ann. "We don't want to miss our bus."

They ran fast and got to the bus just in time. As they were riding home on the bus, Ann asked Hector, "So how was your first day at work?"

"It was great," said Hector. "Mr. Kooper, the pharmacist, is a nice guy."

"Why did you have to go into work so late last night?" asked Nat.

"I had to make a delivery to someone who has cancer from smoking cigarettes," Hector answered. "He sounded like he had a very hard time breathing. He might have emphysema, too."

"Anybody we know?" Ann asked.

"Eh ... no," Hector stammered. "I never met the man who has cancer."

"Who told you he got cancer from smoking?" Ann asked.

"Eh ... I think it was Mr. Kooper," said Hector. Hector began to cough. He was feeling very nervous.

"I heard Flame's father has cancer," said Kate. "It's a good thing you didn't make a delivery to Flame's house. I don't think Ann would like that."

"People shouldn't smoke!" said Nat. "My mother died from cancer because of cigarettes. My father died from emphysema. Now, I am an orphan living with my aunt. I was lucky my aunt was willing to take in her nephew. I hate that stuff!"

Comprehension Questions for Pictures at the Beach

1. Why did Nat say at the end of the story, "I hate that stuff!"

2. Name two animals that are amphibians.

3. Name three animals that are reptiles.

4. What is the difference between reptiles and amphibians?

5. Where do turtles lay their eggs - on land or in water?

6. Where do frogs lay their eggs?

7. Which animal has claws — a frog or a reptile.

8. Name a reptile that has scales, lays its eggs on land, but has no claws?

9. What is a phobia?

10. Why did Ann feel colder in the water than when she came out?

11. As sweat dries, what happens to the temperature of the skin?

12. The <u>esophagus</u> is a tube that connect the _____ to the _____.

13. Where does food go when food goes down the "wrong pipe"?

14. What is a mammal?

15. What is emphysema?

16. Why was Hector nervous when Ann asked if he knew the man who had cancer?

17. Do you think Hector and Ann are going to stay together as boyfriend and girlfriend.   Why?

WORD LIST #7 (com-, con-, ch = k, -ium, -ble, 2-sylable double vowels)

	A	B	C
1	com mon	me di um	chem i cal
2	com mand	pre mi um	chem is try
3	com pare	sta di um	chlo rine
4	com plete	he li um	chlo ride
5	con nect	so di um	char ac ter
6	con fess	cal ci um	me chan ic
7	com bine	a lu min um	stom ach
8	com bined	mag ne si um	mi to chon dri a
9	com bin ing	po tas si um	hy dro chlor ic ac id
10	com bin a tions	au di to ri um	al pha bet
11	com pound	qui et	pam phlet
12	con test	di et	res pi ra tion
13	con fused	fu el	vi ta min
14	con ges tion	flu ids	bub bles
15	con tin ued	ru ined	peb bles
16	con cept	nu cle us	mar ble
17	con cert	min er al	veg e ta bles
18	con cen trate	ce re al	ox y gen
19	con fi dence	bi ol o gy	ox ide
20	con ser va tion	sit u a tion	car bon
21	sub stanc es	vi o lent ly	di ox ide
22	no ticed	nu tri ents	per ox ide
23	pro cess	nu tri tion	hy dro gen
24	in hale	vid e o	di lute
25	ex hale	ster e o	en tire ly
26	o dor less	ra di o	el e ment
27	col or less	po li o	ex per i ment
28	col lect	tongs	en ve lope
29	col lec ted	e qua tion	bal anced

For Reading Only

intestine	altogether
especially	dangerous
zinc	produce
release	produced
released	poisonous
glucose	

WORD LIST #7 (com-, con-, ch = k, -ium, VV, -ble) © Daniel Langer
Concepts: digestion, circulation, respiration; sugar, vitamins/minerals; diagram of cell, mitochondria; elements, atoms, compounds; tests for oxygen, hydrogen, and carbon dioxide; burning magnesium.

Hector Gets a Date with Flame and Ann

The next morning, Hector quickly took a sip of orange juice. He was late for work. After he swallowed the juice, muscles in his esophagus pushed the juice down to his stomach. From the stomach, the juice went into Hector's small intestine. Sugar, water, and vitamin C from the juice went through the walls of his small intestine into his blood vessels. By the time Hector left his house, his heart was pumping the nutrients from his orange juice all over his body.

The street to the pharmacy was uphill, and Hector ran all the way. His heart was racing, pumping needed oxygen and sugar to the muscles in his legs. His muscles needed energy. Tiny mitochondria in each of his muscle cells used the oxygen to slowly burn the sugar and release the energy stored in each sugar molecule. As a result of combining oxygen with sugar, water and carbon dioxide waste were produced and entered his blood stream. His heart pumped the water and the carbon dioxide in his blood to his lungs. Hector was huffing and puffing, taking in oxygen and breathing out carbon dioxide and water vapor. When Hector inhaled, the blood picked up oxygen from his lungs. When he exhaled, his lungs got rid of carbon dioxide and water vapor. After a while, Hector's blood was running out of sugar. His liver began to change fat into sugar. Running to work made Hector lose a little bit of weight.

By the time Hector entered Mr. Kooper's Pharmacy Hector was out of breath. "I'm sorry I'm late, Mr. Kooper," Hector said. "I overslept."

"Hector," Mr. Kooper said. "You can't keep a job if you come late. Be here on time tomorrow. Put these vitamins and minerals on the shelves. After you finish, you have to make some deliveries."

Hector opened a case from the Premium Vitamin and Mineral Company. Hector put some large bottles of vitamin C on the top shelf, and some medium bottles of vitamin B on the second shelf. Then he placed some bottles of calcium pills on the bottom shelf. Hector looked at the label of a mineral bottle. It had minerals, such as iron, copper, magnesium, and potassium.

"Mr. Kooper, what are vitamins and minerals?" Hector asked.

"The cells of your body need vitamins and minerals to do their job. You can get all you need from vegetables and fruit, but some people don't eat all the right things, so they make sure they get all they need from vitamin and mineral pills. But we have talked enough about nutrition. You have to make a delivery to a woman who has polio. She cannot walk, and she needs her blood pressure medicine. She also asked for a pamphlet on a low sodium diet. Tell her that she needs to eat less salt and drink more water and other fluids. She is a very good artist. She wants the delivery to be made to the art studio where she works. When you come back, we have to take an oxygen tank up to Mr. Jones on Godwin Terrace. You were there a few days ago — you know — the man who has cancer."

"Yes, I remember," said Hector. "The man with the pretty daughter. That was my first delivery. Why does Mr. Jones need an oxygen tank?"

"In addition to cancer, Mr. Jones has emphysema. He is having trouble breathing. Years of smoking has ruined his lungs. His lungs are not getting enough oxygen into his blood. His cells do not have enough oxygen to burn sugar for energy. As a result, he gets all out of breath just by sitting up. We have connected a tube to the oxygen tank, with a mask connected to the other end. By breathing in oxygen through the mask, he will have a bit more energy. Without it, he could die."

"I thought sugar is bad for you."

"Sugar is the fuel that your body runs on, but too much sugar is bad for you. We don't need the sugar in candy and soda. It is better to have a balanced diet. When you eat a meal, your small intestine changes some of the nutrients in food to the sugar that your body needs. The starch in bread and cereal is changed in your small intestine to a simple sugar called glucose. Glucose, along with other digested food, is absorbed into the blood stream. The glucose is carried by the blood to your cells. The blood also carries *oxygen* to your cells. Tiny mitochondria in each of your cells combine the sugar with oxygen and change them into carbon dioxide, water, and energy. This process is called respiration. Let me write it down for you."

Respiration

Glucose + Oxygen -------> Carbon dioxide + Water + ENERGY

Hector read what Mr. Kooper wrote: "Respiration: Glucose plus oxygen turns into carbon dioxide, water, and ENERGY."

"The mitochondria are like tiny power plants floating in the cell's cytoplasm," Mr. Kooper explained. "A power plant burns fuel to produce energy. The mitochondria burn glucose to produce energy. Glucose is the fuel. In order for anything to burn, oxygen must combine with the fuel."

"I think I understand the concept of respiration. Respiration is using oxygen to burn glucose for energy. You can't have respiration without oxygen. Part of respiration must include the intake of oxygen by the lungs."

"The lungs also get rid of the waste products of respiration — carbon dioxide and water vapor," Mr. Kooper added. "We inhale oxygen, and exhale carbon dioxide and water vapor. Mr. Jones' lungs do not work right, so he doesn't get enough oxygen."

"I get it," said Hector. "No oxygen, no respiration. No respiration, no energy. No energy — no life."

"You understand the concept of respiration, Hector," said Mr. Kooper, "but we're wasting time, again. No more biology lessons. Go make your delivery, and then come back to the store. We'll take the oxygen tank in the van. I have to make a five minute stop at my auto mechanic. Then we'll take the oxygen tank to Godwin Terrace. After you take it up to Mr. Jones, you can go home."

"Do I have to go to Mr. Jones?" asked Hector. "I don't think I should go back there."

"That's a command!" Mr. Kooper said. "If you want to keep a job, you have to complete all your tasks and do what you are told. And get here on time! Working hard builds character."

* * *

When the door bell rang, Flame turned off the radio, and opened the door.

"I have an oxygen tank for your father," Hector said.

"Bring it into his bedroom," said Flame, "but be quiet. I think he's asleep."

Mr. Jones was sleeping. Tied to a chair was a balloon filled with helium. The balloon said, *GET WELL SOON.*

"Put the tank on the chair," said Flame. "He still has a little oxygen left in the old tank. My mother will connect it when she gets home."

Hector put the oxygen tank on the chair and walked back to the living room.

"Would you like to stay and listen to the stereo, or watch a video?" Flame asked. "We can sit on the couch and have a good time."

"I have to leave in a few minutes," Hector said. "I told Nat I was coming over to his house."

"How can you compare going to Nat's house to staying with me?"

"Well, Samantha, you are much better looking than Nat is," Hector said with a grin. "I'll stay for one song on the stereo."

"I like it when you call me Samantha."
Flame turned on the stereo, and sat down next to Hector.

"I have two tickets to a rock concert at Yankee Stadium for Saturday night." said Flame. "Would you like to take me?"

"I'm not sure," said Hector. "I've never been to a real rock concert before, except for one at the school auditorium, but that doesn't count. I'm so confused. I can't concentrate. I already have a girlfriend."

"Hector," Flame said putting her arms around him. "You know you like me. Confess. I've noticed the way you look at me."

"I do like you, but what will Ann say?"

"You don't need Ann," said Flame. "Have a little confidence in yourself. You've had the same girlfriend for years. It's time to try someone new."

Flames father began to cough again.

"Samantha!!" a voice cried out from the bedroom. "Get me some juice!" He began to cough some more.

"You'd better go now," said Flame. "I have to take care of my father. His lungs have a lot of congestion. The oxygen level in his blood is low. He is very weak. Pick me up at six on Saturday. It's our first date!"

As Hector opened the door to leave, Flame put her arms around him and gave him a soft kiss on his lips. "Pick me up at my house on Saturday at six o'clock," she said. "It's going to be a concert you'll never forget."

That afternoon, Hector went over to Nat's house.

"So how is it going with your new job?" Nat asked.

"Oh, its pretty cool," said Hector. "I had to deliver some oxygen to a man who has cancer and emphysema."

"I bet he's a cigarette smoker," said Nat. "I hate cigarettes."

"He used to smoke a lot," said Hector. "Now he's not getting enough oxygen."

"I can make oxygen with my chemistry kit," said Nat. "Would you like to make some?"

"Sure!" said Hector. "That sounds like fun."

"Oxygen is a pure element," said Nat.

"What's an element?" asked Hector.

"An element is a pure substance made of only one kind of atom. Oxygen is made of only oxygen atoms. Helium is made of Helium atoms. Hydrogen is made of hydrogen atoms. Iron is made of iron atoms. Oxygen, hydrogen, helium, and iron are elements."

"But what is an atom?"

"An atom is smallest bit of an element. All matter — anything that takes up space — is made up of tiny atoms. There are about 109 different *kinds* of atoms, so there are about 109 elements."

"That's crazy," Hector said while scratching his head. "There are millions of different substances on Earth, not just 109! How do we get so many different things from only 109 atoms?"

"By combining atoms," said Nat. "Two or more different atoms combined make a compound. Water is a compound made of two different elements combined. A molecule of water is made of two hydrogen atoms and one oxygen atom: H_2O."

"So a compound is made of two or more different elements combined," said Hector.

"That's right," said Nat. "It's like the 26 letters of the alphabet. By combining letters, we get all the words in the dictionary. Each word is different, even though the same letters are used in different combinations. By combining the 109 elements in different ways, we get all the different substances that exist on the earth. Sodium is an element that reacts violently in water. Chlorine is a poisonous gas. Combine the two together, you get the compound sodium chloride,— common table salt."

"I bet carbon dioxide is a compound, too," said Hector, who was beginning to understand.

"Yes. Carbon dioxide is a compound made of two different elements — carbon and oxygen. A molecule of carbon dioxide is made of one carbon atom and two oxygen atoms — $CO_2.$ We can make carbon dioxide gas with my chemistry kit, too, but first I'd like to make some oxygen."

"Is sugar a compound?"

"Sugar is a compound made of the elements carbon, hydrogen, and oxygen."

Nat opened his chemistry set, took out some chemicals and a rack of test tubes. On the cover of the chemistry kit were the words: "DANGEROUS CHEMICALS. Not to be used by children without an adult."

"Are you sure it's safe to use this?" asked Hector.

"I know what I'm doing," said Nat. "My Dad taught me a lot before he died from smoking cigarettes. First, we put some of this black powder into a test tube," said Nat. "Next, we add some hydrogen peroxide — H_2O_2, a compound that has two hydrogen atoms and two oxygen atoms in each molecule."

"I know what that is," said Hector. "We use hydrogen peroxide to kill germs."

Nat added some hydrogen peroxide into the test tube and it began to bubble."

"See those bubbles?" said Nat. "That's oxygen gas — O_2"

Nat took a thin wooden splint, and lit it with a match. Then he blew out the flame, and the wooden splint was glowing red hot, but not on fire. He put the splint back into the test tube, and the wooden splint lit up again. He took the splint out, blew out the flame, put the splint back into the test tube, and the flame came back. "That's oxygen all right. Oxygen is needed for fire. Pure oxygen will make a glowing splint light up again."

The doorbell rang. It was Ann and Kate.

"Take a look at this, girls," said Hector. "This is cool."

Nat added some more hydrogen peroxide to a black powder in the test tube, and it began to bubble. He put a glowing splint in the tube and the splint caught on fire.

"I know what that is," said Ann. "That's oxygen. Fires need oxygen. I saw that in my science book."

"When anything burns," said Nat, "oxygen combines with the fuel. When that happens, energy is released. When we burn wood, the energy is in the form of heat and light. When our muscles use oxygen to burn glucose, the energy is in the form of heat and muscle energy."

"Hector had to deliver a tank of oxygen today to someone who has cancer," said Nat.

"I heard Flame's father has cancer," said Ann. "This man doesn't have a daughter named Flame, does he?"

"Eh...He he does have a daughter," Hector stammered. "Her name is Samantha."

"Good," said Ann. "I wouldn't want to catch you in Flame's house. She is not a character you can trust."

"Let's make another compound," said Nat.

Nat took his chemistry kit to the kitchen sink. He took a thin strip of metal and held it with some metal tongs. "This is the element magnesium," he said. "It is a metal made of only magnesium atoms. Now watch what happens when we burn it."

Nat lit the magnesium ribbon and it burned with a very bright white light.

"Look away," said Nat. "The bright light can hurt your eyes."

The magnesium turned from a silver metal color to a white powder. "This is no longer pure magnesium metal," Nat continued. "When we burned it, oxygen atoms in the air combined with the magnesium atoms to form a compound called magnesium oxide. We have formed a new substance. When we use heat to combine magnesium, with oxygen, we get a new substance — the compound magnesium oxide:

Magnesium + Oxygen -------> Magnesium oxide
$$2Mg + O_2 \longrightarrow 2MgO$$

Two elements combine to form a compound. That's a chemical change. In a chemical change, a new substance is formed."

"Wow!" said Kate. "That magnesium lit up the whole room."

"Not as much as you light up my life," Nat said, looking into Kate's eyes.

"And look!" said Ann. "The magnesium oxide is a white powder! We started with magnesium, a silver metal, and used heat to add oxygen, a gas, and we ended up with a white powder. The compound, magnesium oxide, is very different from the two elements it is made of. That really *is* a chemical change!"

"Now, for my next experiment!" said Nat. "In the last two experiments, we made fire. This time we shall put out fire!"

Nat put a short candle into a beaker, and lit the candle. Next, he put some marble pebbles into another beaker and added some dilute hydrochloric acid. Gas bubbles appeared in the beaker. He used some rubber tubing to collect the gas in a jar. Then he poured the gas over the candle, and the fire went out.

"Guess what gas made the candle go out?" asked Nat.

"Is it oxygen?" asked Kate. "Oxygen is a gas."

"No," said Ann. "Oxygen makes things burn! This gas put *out* the fire!"

"I know!" Hector exclaimed. "Carbon dioxide! Carbon dioxide puts out fire!"

"That's right!" said Nat.

Ann said "Let me give you a kiss, Hector, for being so smart."

"Any more experiments, Nat?" asked Hector. "This is fun, especially when Ann gives me a kiss.

"I have one more," said Nat. "I shall make for you some hydrogen gas."

Nat added some zinc and hydrochloric acid to a flask. The acid began to bubble. Nat put a cork that had some rubber tubing on top of the flask, and collected the hydrogen gas in a test tube. Nat then lit a match to the test tube and there was a "pop". The inside of the test tube was now wet with water.

"How did that happen?" asked Kate. "Where did the water come from?"

"When we lit the match to the test tube, the oxygen in the air combined with the hydrogen in the test tube to form water," said Nat. "Water is a compound made of the elements hydrogen and oxygen. Let me write out the equation.

$$\text{Hydrogen} + \text{Oxygen} \text{-------}> \text{Water}$$
$$2H_2 \quad + \quad O_2 \quad \text{-------}> \quad 2H_2O$$

A water molecule (H_2O) is made of two hydrogen atoms and one oxygen atom."

"Why is oxygen written as O_2?" asked Kate.

"The atoms in the oxygen molecule exist in pairs. That is why we write the oxygen molecule as O_2. The same is true for hydrogen. The atoms of the hydrogen molecule exist in pairs, so hydrogen is H_2."

"Then why did you put a '2' in front of the hydrogen and the water molecules?" asked Kate.

"The law of conservation of matter says that matter cannot be created or destroyed," said Nat. "In a chemical reaction, atoms can form new combinations, but the atoms you start with have to be the same as the atoms you end up with. We started with an oxygen molecule that had two atoms of oxygen. The water molecule has only one atom of oxygen, so we put a two in front of the water molecule ($2H_2O$). Now we have two water molecules, which has two oxygen atoms altogether. The oxygen atoms are balanced: we start with two and end up with two."

"But then Hydrogen atoms are not balanced," said Kate. "Two water molecules ($2H_2O$) have **four** hydrogen atoms (2X2).

"I get it," said Ann. "You put a two in front of the hydrogen molecule ($2H_2$), so you start with four hydrogen atoms and you end up with four hydrogen atoms."

"That's right," said Nat. "When you write a chemical equation this way, you start and end with the same number and kinds of atoms on each side of the arrow. The law of conservation of matter is not violated. But the atoms are combined in new ways. That is what makes a chemical change — you end up with different molecules, even though the atoms themselves are the same."

"That is cool," said Ann.

"Now let's have a contest," said Nat. "I collected some extra test tubes of each gas. Here are three test tubes with three different gasses. Each gas is odorless and colorless. Can you guess what each is? The winner gets a prize."

Nat lit a match and put it near the mouth of the first test tube. There was a pop, and water collected inside the lining of the test tube.. "What was in test tube #1?" Nat asked.

"I know," said Kate. "Hydrogen."

"That's right," said Nat. "Kate is winning. Now for test tube #2." Nat lit a candle and poured the gas in the test tube over the candle. The candle went out.

"Oxygen," said Hector.

"No!" said Ann. "Oxygen would make the candle burn brighter, not put it out! It's carbon dioxide!"

"Correct!" said Nat. "Carbon dioxide puts out fire. Ann and Kate are tied.
Now for test tube #3." Nat lit a wooden splint, blew it out, put it into the test tube, and the splint lit up again."

"That's easy" said Kate. "Oxygen!"

"Correct," said Nat. "Kate wins the contest."

'What's the prize?" asked Kate.

"The winner gets to kiss Nat, the science cat," Nat replied with a grin.

Kate walked over to Nat and gave him a long kiss on the lips.

"You see," said Nat. "It pays to know your science."

"Don't feel bad, Hector," said Ann. "I have a prize for us." Ann walked over and sat down next to Hector.

"What prize do you have for us?" Hector asked.

Ann put her arms around Hector, and handed him an envelope. Hector opened the envelope and took out two tickets. "What's this for?" he asked.

"Two tickets to the concert at Yankee Stadium on Saturday night," said Ann, as she gave Hector a quick kiss.

"Oh, Hector," said Nat. "You're so lucky! I wanted to go to that concert!"

"Don't feel bad," said Kate, putting her arm around Nat. "Ann and I got tickets for the four of us."

"Cool!" said Nat.

"A date for for the four of us!" said Ann. "I can't wait!"

Hector thought about the date he had with Flame to to the same concert on the same night. "How did I get myself into this situation?" he said to himself.

Comprehension Questions

1. What tube in your body pushes food from the mouth to the stomach?

2. After the stomach, food enters the _____ _____.

3. Digested food enters the blood stream through the walls of the _____ _____.

4. What gas does your body need in order to burn glucose?

5. The cells in your body burn glucose in order to make

6. What part of the cell burns glucose to produce energy?

7. What three things are produced when glucose combines with oxygen?

8. When you inhale, what does the blood pick up from the lungs

9. When you exhale, what two gases does your blood get rid of?

10. Hector's muscles need sugar and oxygen to produce _____.

11. When Hector's blood ran low on sugar, his liver changed _____ to sugar.

12. When Hector ran, why did his breathing increase and his heart beat faster?

13. Mr. Jones has emphysema. He has very little energy. Why?

14. Your small intestine changes starch in bread and cereal into _____.

15. What carries blood and oxygen to your cells?

16. What is respiration?

17. What do the mitochondria in your cells do?

18. In order for anything to burn, what element must combine with the fuel?

19. What are the two waste products of respiration?

20. Draw a diagram of a cell.

21. Why did Hector tell Mr. Kooper that he didn't think he should go back to Mr. Kooper's apartment?

22. Why does Mr. Jones need an oxygen tank?

23. What gas was used to fill the get-well balloon?

24. What is an element

25. Give four examples of elements

26. What is an atom?

27. What is a compound?

28. Give three examples of compounds:

29. Water is made of which two elements?

30 Hydrogen peroxide made of? _____ and _____

How is hydrogen peroxide different from water?

31. What is carbon dioxide made of?

32. What compound is formed when you burn magnesium?

33. Describe a test for oxygen.

34. Describe a test for carbon dioxide

35. Describe a test for hydrogen

36. Define the law of conservation of matter

37. What was Kate's prize for winning the contest?

38. Why did Hector say, "How did I get myself into this situation?"
Explain Hector's problem.

39. What do you think will happen on Saturday night, the night of the concert?

WORD LIST (-sion, -cious, eu = /oo/)

-sion preceded by a vowel = /zjun/, as in vision, explosion.
-sion preceded by a consonant = /tion/, as in mission, tension.

	A	B	C
1	vi sion	mis sion	de li cious
2	tel e vi sion	ad mis sion	lus cious
3	su per vi sion	per mis sion	spa cious
4	in ci sion	in ter mis sion	gra cious
5	de ci sion	ten sion	a tro cious
6	di vi sion	ses sion	fer o cious
7	con fu sion	pas sion	vi cious
8	con clu sion	im pres sion	pre cious
9	il lu sion	de pres sion	sus spi cious
10	ex plo sion	con fes sion	con cious
11	oc ca sion	com pas sion	un con cious
12	trans fu sion	pro fes sion	con cious ness
13	lens	pro fes sion al	e lec tron
14	cor ne a	per cus sion	e lec tric
15	i ris	ex pres sion	e lec tric al
16	pu pil	sus pen sion	e lec tric i ty
17	ret in a	por tion	stat ic
18	op tic nerve	sec tion	mag net
19	at tract	con di tion	mag net ic
20	re pel	in ter rup tion	e lec tro mag net ic
21	pro ton	dis trac tion	spec trum
22	e lec tron	feud	in fra red
23	med i cal	neu tron	ul tra vi o let
24	co ma	neu tral	pos si ble
25	or di nar y	neu ron	vis i ble
26	pos i tive	ma neu ver	in vis i ble
27	neg a tive	am a teur	par ti cle
28	neg a tive ly	in ter pret	e mer gen cy

For Reading Only

headache
cruise
stretcher
especially

disbelief
wavelength
facinating
Electromagnetism

WORD LIST #8 (-sion, -cious, eu = /oo/) © Daniel Langer
Concepts: Atom; electricity, electric charge, electromagnets, electromagnetic spectrum and wavelengths, television and radio waves; danger of playing with chemicals; anatomy and function of the eye.

A Vicious Fight at the Concert

"I have to go home, now," said Kate, as she passed her comb through her hair.

"Wait," said Nat. "Let me have your comb for a minute." Nat tore up some paper into tiny pieces. Then he placed the comb next to the papers, and the papers stuck to the comb.

"I know that trick," said Kate.

"That's no trick," said Nat. "That's static electricity. Atoms have tiny electrons that spin around a nucleus made of protons and neutrons. Let me draw you a picture of a helium atom:

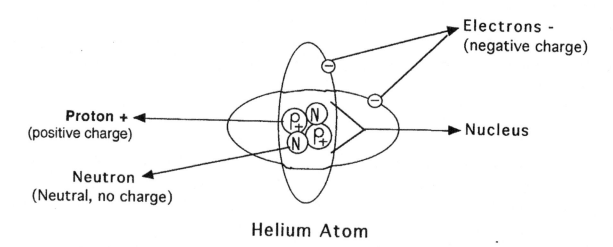

Helium Atom

Each electron has a negative electric charge balanced by the positive charge of the protons in the atom's nucleus. Negative charges attract positive charges. Opposite charges attract. Like charges repel. When you comb your hair, you rub off some electrons you're your hair onto the comb. The extra negative electrons in the comb attract the positive charges in the atoms of the paper."

"Do electrons have anything to do with electricity?" Kate asked.

"Yes. Electricity is the movement of electrons," said Nat. "Did you ever notice that a battery has a positive (+) side and a negative (–) side? Each side is called a terminal. Well, the negative terminal of a battery has lots of extra electrons with negative charges. Because these electrons have like charges, they repel each other. The positive terminal attracts the negatively charged electrons. Connect a wire to each terminal, and electrons flow through the wire from the negative terminal to the positive terminal. Now watch this."

Nat went into his room and returned with a battery, a wire, and an iron nail. He wrapped the wire around the iron nail and connected each end of the wire to the ends of a battery. Then he picked up some paper clips with the iron nail.

"I know what that is," said Hector. "That's an electromagnet. How does the nail turn into a magnet?"

"I'm not sure," said Nat. "Somehow, electrons moving through a wire produce a magnetic force. Moving a wire through a magnetic field makes the electrons in the wire move, producing electricity. Electricity can produce magnetic force, and a magnetic force can produce electricity. Electric force and magnetic force are related."

"Well, that's very interesting," Kate said while taking back her comb, "but I still have to go."

"Stay a little longer and have some apple pie with vanilla ice cream," said Nat.

"That sounds delicious," said Kate, "but I promised my mom to be home for dinner."

"What about you, Ann?" Nat asked. "Have some pie before you say bye!"

"That's very gracious of you," said Ann, "but I have to go home, too."

"I think I'll stick around with Nat," said Hector. "I can't pass on anything as luscious as apple pie with vanilla ice cream. Also, I have to talk to Nat about something."

"OK," Ann said to Hector. "Pick me up at six on Saturday night. I can't wait to go out with you to the rock concert at Yankee Stadium."

Hector scratched his head. He already had a date with Flame to the same concert. Hector had to think quickly. "I can't pick you up at six," he said. "I'm working late on Saturday."

"How late are you working?" asked Ann. "The drug store closes at seven on Saturday."

"I'm working until seven," he replied.

"I don't want to be late," said Ann. "Can't you get off early?"

"No," said Hector, thinking that he would be able to get out of the situation.

"Why don't you give one of the tickets to Hector?" said Nat. "That way Hector can meet us at our seats."

"Great idea," said Ann. "You might miss a few band sessions, but the concert is long. Here's your ticket. The seat number is marked. We'll meet you at the concert. Then we can all go home together."

Hector took the ticket and put it in his pocket. He felt nervous, and his head was pounding. He was getting a tension headache.

After the girls left, Nat made two portions of pie and ice cream, and gave one portion to Hector. "

Hector took a bite of the pie and licked his lips. "This really is delicious," he said.

Nat turned on the television to the Yankee game. The Yankees were playing in Texas.

"How is it possible for us to hear and see a game played in Texas while sitting in New York eating pie?" asked Hector.

"First, think about this," said Nat. "How is it possible for the light from the television set ten feet away able to reach our eyes?"

"Light from the television travels to our eyes," said Hector. "But what exactly is light?"

"Light is an electromagnetic wave of energy," said Nat. "Television signals are radio waves. Radio waves are electromagnetic waves, just like ordinary light, but in a color we can't see."

"How do we get different colors?" asked Hector.

"Electromagnetic waves come in different wavelengths. Just as the distance between ocean waves can be long or short, electromagnetic wavelengths can be long or short. Blue light has a short wavelength, and red light has a long wavelength.

BLUE LIGHT — short wavelength

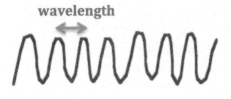

RED LIGHT — long wavelength

We can only see a small portion of all the possible electromagnetic wavelengths. Most electromagnetic wavelengths are invisible. Visible light is only a small part of the electro-magnetic spectrum. If the wavelength is too short or too long, we can't see it. We cannot see infrared light or radio waves because they have very long wavelengths. Neither can we see ultraviolet light or x-rays, because they have very short wavelengths.

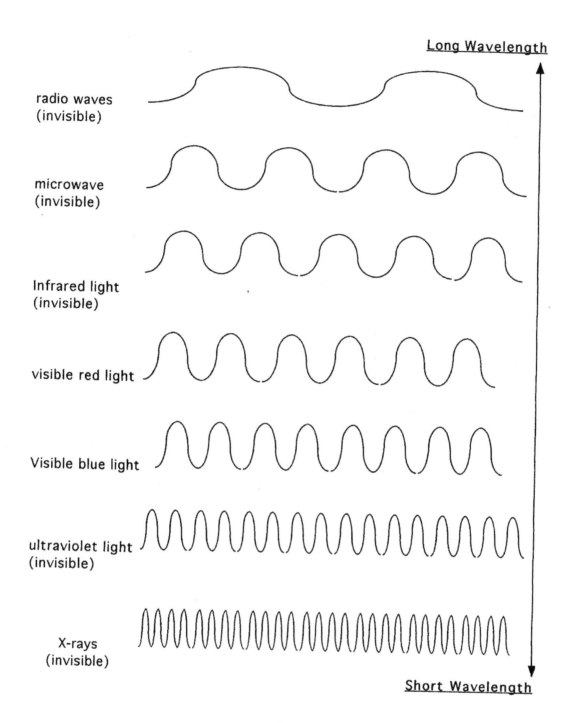

Long Wavelength

radio waves
(invisible)

microwave
(invisible)

Infrared light
(invisible)

visible red light

Visible blue light

ultraviolet light
(invisible)

X-rays
(invisible)

Short Wavelength

"What does all this have to do with my question?" Hector asked. "How can we watch a live Yankee game all the way from Texas?"

"The television camera changes sound and light into patterns of electricity. The television station changes these electrical patterns into patterns of radio waves. Radio waves travel at the speed of light. The television set changes the radio waves back to patterns of electricity. These are then turned into light and sound by the television. Light and sound then travels from the TV to your eyes and ears. In your eyes and ears, nerve cells, called neurons, send signals to your brain.

sound waves ---> patterns of electricity ----> radio waves ----> patterns of waves ---->
electricity in TV ---->**Sound waves**

Light waves ------> patterns of electricity ---------> radio waves -------> patterns of
electricity in TV --------> **Light waves**

So radio waves from Texas are sent to the Bronx so you can watch the Yankee game on
your TV."

"That's facinating," said Hector, as he finished eating his pie. "The pie was delicious,
Nat. Thanks."

"Anything for a good friend," said Nat, "but you don't look too happy. Your face has a
sad expression."

"I have a confession to make," said Hector. "Can you keep a secret?"

"My lips are sealed," said Nat.

"OK, I'll tell you," Hector said. "I told you I had to deliver medicine to a man who has
cancer. Well, the man is Flame's father."

"Wow! Are you in trouble! I thought you said his daughter's name is Samantha?" Nat
asked.

"Samantha is Flame's *real* name," Hector replied.

"I don't think Ann is going to like that," said Nat.

"I have another confession to make. When I was leaving, Flame kissed me."

"Ann is *really* not going to like that."

"It gets worse," said Nat. "Flame told me to pick her up at six on Saturday. She has
tickets to the concert at Yankee Stadium for the two of us."

"Oh, man," said Nat. "You are in *deep* trouble. Ann would never give you permission
to go out with another girl, especially Flame! The two of them have had a vicious feud for a
long time. They are always snapping on each other. Whenever they get together, they act
like two ferocious female lions. If Ann finds out, there is going to be an explosion!"

"I don't know what to do," said Hector. "I feel so much confusion. I can't make a
decision."

"You have to make a decision," said Nat. "You can't go out with both of them!"

"When Flame kissed me," said Hector. "I felt a strong feeling of passion. She is so
fine!"

"Her father is dying of cancer and emphysema, and she's kissing at the door!" Nat
said in disbelief. She does not give the impression that she has any compassion for her
father."

"She cares about her father a lot," Hector said, "but I am the man. She can't resist
me."

"I don't know," said Nat. "She is making passes at a boy while her father is in the
bedroom dying. What kind of a person is that?"

"She's not that bad," said Hector. "I guess it is very hard for her, and she needs some
distraction from her troubles."

"Don't you care about Ann?" asked Nat.

"I like Ann a lot," said Hector. "She has always been there for me. When I got a suspension from school for fighting, Ann came to visit me every day after school to cheer me up. I remember the occasion when my father came out of prison. I was very upset. My mom wouldn't take him back. I wanted my family to be together, but it didn't happen. Ann helped me get through that. She is the first girl I have ever kissed. I love Ann, but Samantha is so fine. I am so confused. I don't know what to do."

"Tell Flame you can't go out with her," said Nat.

"I can't do that," said Hector. "She is really looking forward to going with me. She needs a break from her troubles at home. Sometimes the expression on her face is so sad. Going out with me may help her get out of her depression."

"So what are you going to do?" asked Nat.

"I think I'll pick up Samantha early," said Nat. "Ann thinks I'm working late, and she isn't expecting me to be at the concert until later. I'll tell Samantha I have to go to the bathroom, and then meet you guys at the seat. Then I'll tell Ann I have to go to the bathroom, or to pick up a soda, and then go back to Samantha. I can maneuver back and forth like that for a while. Then I'll tell Ann I have a tension headache, and that I have to leave early. You and Kate can take Ann home."

"This is not going to work," said Nat. "You're going to get caught in a lie."

"I can't think of another way to get out of this situation," said Hector. "By the way, can I borrow your chemistry set? I want to show off what I can do to Samantha."

"OK," said Nat. "But be careful. You're not supposed to use this set without adult supervision."

* * *

Hector picked Flame up a six on the evening of the concert. They took the train to Yankee Stadium. Flame handed the man at the gate two tickets for admission to the concert.

When they got to their seats, a band began playing.

"This music is great," said Hector. "It's much better listening to professionals instead of the amateurs that play at school auditorium."

"I like the man playing percussion," said Flame. "He plays the drums with a lot of passion."

After an hour, there was an intermission. Hector said, "I have to go to the bathroom." Hector was glad he was able to go to Ann without making Flame suspicious.

Hector ran up the steps. He looked at the other ticket in his pocket. The seats were a few sections away from his seat with Flame. He ran and slipped over some spilled beer, and fell down. He got up, and limped to the seat next to where Ann, Kate, and Nat were sitting.

"You finally made it," said Ann, giving Hector a kiss.

"Mr. Kooper made me work late," said Hector.

"Too bad you missed the last band," said Kate.

"The guy on percussion was as hot as a flame," Nat said with a sly grin. Hector looked at Nat hard, as if to say, *don't give up my secret*!

The intermission came to an end, and a new band began playing. After about ten minutes, Hector said, "I have to go to the bathroom." Hector ran up the steps. He was breathing faster in order to get more oxygen so that his muscles could burn sugar for energy. When he got to Flame's seat, he was all out of breath.

"You took a long time," said Flame. "What happened? Did you get lost? And why are you out of breath?"

"I couldn't find our seats," Hector replied. "I was looking in the wrong section. I was running all around the stadium."

"Well, now *I* have to go to the bathroom," said Flame. "I'll be right back."

When Flame got to the women's bathroom, she saw Ann and Kate outside.

"What are you doing here with Kate — couldn't get a date?" said Flame

"I'm here with Hector!" said Ann.

"Your nose grows when you tell a lie," said Flame. "I didn't think your nose could get any bigger."

Ann looked straight at Flame and said, "You had better not put your nose near your armpit. One whiff of your armpit and your whiskers will fall out!"

"That was dumb," said Flame. "You're so dumb you can't even do addition or division. I like the title of your new book. It's called, *Everything I Know,* by Ann. It's one page long, and the page has only one word on it — *Duhh....*"

"At least I'm not dirty, like you," Ann snapped. "You're so dirty, you lose ten pounds every time you take a shower. They don't let you go to the gym any more, because every time you takes a shower, you clog up the drain."

"Are you guys ever going to end your feud and stop snapping?" asked Kate. "This kind of behavior is atrocious."

"Flame started," said Ann. "I didn't ask her bad breath to get in my face."

"If you snap on me like that one more time, I am going to punch you in your big, fat mouth," said Flame. "Maybe you won't look so strange, if I rearrange your face!"

Just then the band began playing Kate's favorite song. Kate pulled Ann by the arm and said, "That's my favorite song. Let's go back to our seats. I don't want to miss the conclusion of the show."

Hector had just sat down next to Nat, as Ann and Kate got back to their seats. Ann was upset.

"What's wrong?" asked Hector.

"We bumped into Flame outside the bathroom," said Kate. "Ann and Flame were snapping at each other."

Hector turned green. "Let me go get you a soda," he said to Ann. "I think there is a long line, so it may take awhile."

Hector rushed back to his seat next to Flame. "Where were you?" asked Flame. "I bumped into your ugly ex-girlfriend."

"I went to look for you," Hector said. "Look, let me show you a trick."

"You can do illusions?" Flame asked.

"This is no illusion," said Hector. "This is chemistry. It's real. I am going to make some hydrogen gas and make it pop."

Hector had a bag with some of Nat's chemicals. He took out a jar that said, **Concentrated hydrochloric acid. Dangerous. Dilute by adding a small amount to water before using.** Hector was holding the jar of acid, when he looked up and saw Bubba standing over him.

"*What are you doing here sitting next to my girl?!!*" Bubba said in an angry tone.

"What does it look like, big boy?" Hector answered. "We're on a date!"

"Don't call me 'Big Boy' you little punk," said Bubba. "Flame is *my* girl. You had better sit somewhere else!"

"So where are you going to sit?" said Hector. "You can't even fit in the chair, and you're too cheep to buy a ticket for good seats like these."

"Talk about cheap," said Bubba. "Your jailbird father is so cheap that for his honeymoon, he took your mother on a cruise — in a bathtub!"

Hector was very angry. He didn't like anyone snapping on his father, especially about his dad's jail time. Hector stood up and pushed Bubba.

"You trying to push me, you little punk!" Bubba picked Hector up, turned him upside down, and threw him to the ground headfirst. Hector tried to break his fall with his hands. The bottle of acid smashed as Hector hit his head on the edge of a cement step. Hector was unconscious, unable to feel the acid that had splashed into his eyes.

Police took Bubba away, as security guards carried Hector in a stretcher to an ambulance.

Ann had been looking around for Hector, when she saw the security guards carrying someone on a stretcher. "Doesn't that look like Hector?" she asked.

Nat stood up and looked. "Hey, that *is* Hector!"

"Oh, no!" cried Ann. "What happened to my boyfriend!"

* * *

Ann, Nat, and Kate took the bus to the hospital. When they arrived, Flame was already waiting outside the emergency room."

"What are you doing here?" Ann asked Flame.

"Hector took me to the concert, so they let me ride in the ambulance," said Flame. "My father is dying, and now my new boyfriend is in the hospital. I can't take it any more!" Flame began to cry.

"Hector took *you* to the concert?" Ann asked. "He said he had to meet me at the concert, because he said he had to work late. No wonder he was running back and forth so much! He was running from me to you, Flame."

Samantha looked hard at Ann, and said, "My name is not Flame, you little ... No, I had better not snap at you. This is not the time for snapping. Hector was knocked unconscious when his head hit the cement step. He has acid burns in both eyes. We should not be fighting with each other at a time like this. Flame is my nickname. My friends call me Samantha."

"Samantha?" Ann asked. "Hector said he had to make deliveries to Samantha's father. Is that you?"

"Yes," said Flame. "My father is dying."

"I'm sorry," said Ann.

"Pardon the interruption," said Nat, "but let's see if we can slip past the nurse's station to see Hector."

When the nurse wasn't looking, they all walked quickly inside.

The emergency room was spacious. There was room for forty beds. Hector was in the first bed. He was lying unconscious with bandages over both eyes.

"What happened?" Nat asked a doctor who was standing nearby.

"He wasn't conscious when the ambulance brought him in." said the doctor. "He is in a coma. He hit his head hard, and there was some bleeding, but he does not need a blood transfusion."

"Will he be all right?" Ann asked with tears in her eyes.

"His condition is very serious," said the doctor. "If he gains consciousness, he will live, but he has bad acid burns in both eyes. For some stupid reason, he was carrying a bottle of concentrated hydrochloric acid when he got into a vicious fight."

"What part of his eyes got burned," asked Nat.

"Do you know the parts of the eye?" asked the doctor.

"I do," said Nat. "When I grow up, I want to be part of the medical profession. It will be my mission to heal the sick"

THE EYE

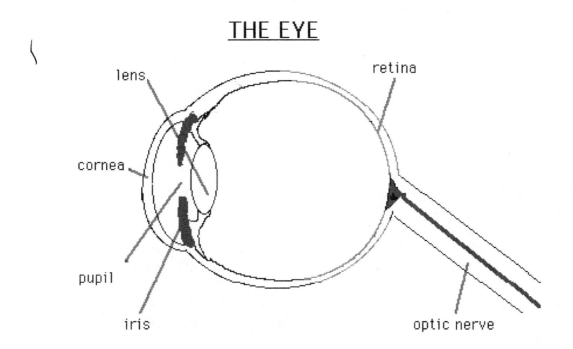

PARTS OF THE EYE

Cornea — the clear outer cover of the front of the eye.
Iris – the colored muscle in the eye that controls the size of the pupil.
Pupil — the hole in the middle of the iris through which light enters the inner eye.
Lens — lying behind the pupil, the lens focuses light onto the retina.
Retina — made of light sensitive neurons at the back of the eye. The lens produces an upside–down image on the retina.
Optic Nerve — carries signals from the retina to the brain. The brain interprets these signals as sight, and flips the image right side up

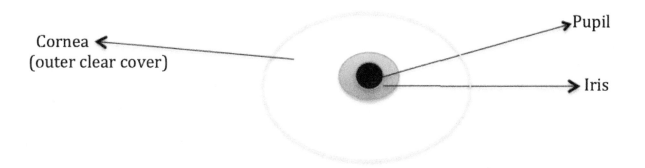

Cornea
(outer clear cover)

Pupil

Iris

"Some glass made an incision in his left eye. That will heal. The serious thing is that he has burns on his cornea — in both eyes. The cornea is the clear outer cover of the eye. There is no harm to his iris, the colored part of the eye that opens and closes to control the amount of light entering the eye. His lens is okay, the part of the eye that focuses light. The neurons in the retina at the back of the eye are in good condition. But If scar tissue develops on the cornea, he will lose his vision. If the cornea is not clear, light cannot enter the eye. Vision is precious. Kids should not play with acid!" The doctor walked away angry.

"It's all my fault," said Nat. "I let him borrow my chemistry set."

"Doesn't that set say not to be used by kids without adult supervision?" asked Kate.

"It does," said Nat. "I thought I knew what I was doing. I should never have let him use it. Hector may never see again."

<u>Comprehension Questions</u>

The atom

1. Name the three main particles of the atom (see diagram of helium atom).

2. Which two particles are found in the nucleus?

3. What part of the atom spins around the nucleus?

4. Which particle has a negative charge?

5. Which particle has a positive charge?

6. Which particle is neutral, having no charge.

7. Do opposite charges attract or repel?

8. Do like charges attract or repel?

9. Draw a diagram of a helium atom.

Electromagnetism

10. Why did the paper stick to the comb? Explain.

11. What is electricity?

12. What is an electromagnet?

13. How are radio waves and light waves alike?

14. Which has a shorter wavelength, red light or blue light?

15. Which has a longer wavelength, radio waves or visible light?

The Story

16. What secret did Hector tell Nat?

17. Why did Hector have a tension headache?

18. How does Hector plan to keep his date with Flame and with Ann?

19. Why does Hector like Ann?

20. Why does Hector like Flame?

21. Which girl do you think Hector likes best — Flame or Ann? Why?

22. Why is it dangerous to play with chemicals?

23. What happened to Hector's eyes?

The eye

24. What is the clear outer cover of the eye called?

25. What is the iris?

26. What is the pupil of the eye?

27. What does the lens do?

28. What is the retina?

29. What carries signals from the retina to the brain?

30. What did Bubba say that got Hector so upset?

31. What did Bubba do to Hector?

32. Do you think Hector will ever be able to see again? Why?

WORD LIST #9 (-age, -ent, -ant, -ual, -ture, -cial, -tial, -cient, -tient)

	A	B	C
1	cab bage	un u su al	lent
2	lug gage	vi su al	vi o lent
3	gar bage	an nu al	ex cel lent
4	vil lage	sex u al	dent
5	im age	grad u al	ac ci dent
6	mes sage	in di vid u al	e vent
7	do sage	in tel lec tu al	cur rent
8	ad van tage	sen su al	ur gent
9	dis ad vant age	spir i tu al	per cent
10	dam aged	e qual	dif fer ent
11	band age	spe cial	mo ment
12	band ag es	so cial	oint ment
13	bev er age	cru cial	ar gu ment
14	voy age	of fi cial	treat ment
15	saus age	com mer cial	im prove ment
	cour age	ar ti fi cial	e quip ment
16	en cour age	pa tient	mag ni f i cent
17	volts	im pa tient	in tel li gent
18	volt age	an cient	trans lu cent
19	sta men	suf fi cient	pro duce
20	pis til	na ture	o paque
21	an ther	pic ture	o be di ent
22	pol len	de par ture	trans plant
23	stig ma	ad ven ture	im por tant
24	o va r y	ma ture	as sist ant
25	o vule	im ma ture	mal lig nant
26	sob bed	meas ured	sig nif i cant
27	sob bing	re vived	ig no rant
28	who's = who is	re stored	re sis tance
29	whose	tu mor	med i ca tion
30	se ries	spe cif ic	suf fo ca tion
31	par al lel	cor ne al	con cus sion
32			al co hol

For Reading Only

circuit

WORD LIST #9 (-age, -ent, -ant, -ual, -ture, -cial, -tial, -cient, -tient)
Concepts: Electric shock to restore heartbeat; voltage, resistance, current, series circuit, parallel circuit; corneal transplant; transparent, translucent, opaque; anatomy and function of flower; liver; kidney.

The Patient

Hector's heart monitor began beeping loudly. The screen showed a straight line. Ann ran to the nurse's station.

"Help!" she cried. "I think his heart has stopped!"

A doctor and a nurse ran to his side.

"He has no pulse!" shouted the nurse. "His heart has stopped beating!"

"Get ready to shock him," said the doctor.

The nurse brought some electrical equipment to shock Hector's heart back to life.

"Clear!" the doctor shouted. Hector's body jerked as electricity flowed through his body.

"Still no heartbeat!" said the nurse.

"Again!" said the doctor. "Clear!"

Hector's body jerked again, but there was still no pulse. There should be a pulse for each heart beat. Whenever the heart beats, blood rushes through the arteries and a pulse can be felt.

"Increase the voltage!" said the doctor.

"Voltage increased," said the nurse.

"Clear!" said the doctor. Hector's body jerked again, but this time, the monitor showed a heartbeat.

"We have a pulse!" said the nurse.

"That was a close one," the doctor said to Ann. "It is a good thing you called me over quickly, young lady. You saved the boy's life. His heart responded when we increased the voltage.

The increased voltage was able to produce a heart beat. You kids had better step outside, now. You are really not allowed in the emergency room. His mother should be here in a few minutes."

"Can I stay with him until his mother comes?" asked Ann.

"OK," said the doctor. "Just until his mother arrives. The rest of you have to go to the waiting room."

Nat, Kate, and Flame went to the waiting room. They sat down next to a man with two pieces of luggage. He had a serious condition. He had just come from South America to get the excellent medical treatment offered in a United States hospital. He had taken a cab straight from the airport to the emergency room.

Flame began to cry on Nat's shoulder. "Hector almost died!" she sobbed.

"He's alive," said Nat. "That's the most important thing. The electric shock revived his heart."

"The doctor told the nurse to increase the voltage," said Kate. "What exactly is voltage?"

"Voltage is the force that pushes electrons through a wire," said Nat. "Voltage is measured in volts. The socket in the wall has 120 volts. A battery has 1.5 volts. The greater the voltage, the greater the current."

"Current?" asked Kate

"Electric current is the number of electrons flowing through a wire in each second. Current is the rate of electric flow through a wire."

"I don't get it," said Kate.

"Let me explain it this way," said Nat. "If you press the trigger of a power water gun with more force, more water comes out. The current of water is stronger."

"I get it, now," said Kate. "If you have more voltage pushing the electrons, more electric current will flow through the wire."

"That's right," said Nat. "The greater the force (voltage), the greater the current. That's why you need two batteries to light a flashlight. One battery does not have enough voltage, and therefore not enough current to light the bulb."

"I have a question," said Kate. "Doesn't a 100 watt light bulb use more electricity than a 60 watt light bulb?"

"Yes," said Nat. "A 100 watt bulb uses more current than a 60 watt bulb."

"But how is that possible?" asked Kate. "All the outlets in the house have the same 120 volts. How can a 100 watt lamp use more current than a 60 watt lamp, if the voltage is the same?"

"The voltage is the same," said Nat, "But the resistance is not the same. A thin wire has more resistance than a thick wire."

"Thick wire, thin wire — what's the difference?"

"Imagine you are standing on the side of a three-way highway watching the cars pass by," said Nat. "There are a lot of cars, but the traffic is flowing smoothly. 400 cars pass by you each minute. Then there is an accident. Two lanes are closed. The closed lanes cause more resistance to traffic. Fewer cars can pass through, so the traffic rate drops to 40 cars per minute."

"I get it," said Kate. "A thick wire is like a three-lane highway. The electrons moving through the wire are like the cars. A thin wire is like a one-lane road — fewer electrons can get through each second. More electricity flows through a thick wire than through a thin wire."

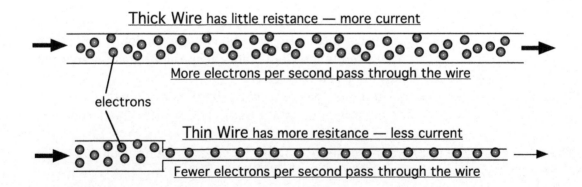

"Yes," said Nat. "I like intelligent girls. A thick wire can carry more current than a thin wire. Thin wires have more resistance than thick wires. The more resistance, the lower the current. A 60-watt bulb has more resistance than a 100-watt bulb. That's why a 60-watt bulb uses less electricity. Fewer electrons per second flow through a 60 watt bulb than through a 100 watt bulb."

"Now I get it," said Kate. "If you look at an old light bulb, you can see the thin wire that lights up when electricity flows through it. But I have a question. My mom always tells me to shut lights when I leave the house to save on our electric bill. If each lamp has a bulb with a thin wire, wouldn't that make for more resistance and less electricity?"

"They would, if the lamps in your house were hooked up in a series circuit, like in some Christmas tree lighting, but the outlets in your house are hooked up in parallel circuits. A Parallel circuit adds extra paths for the electricity to flow through. The more lamps you put on, the more paths open up, and the more electric current flows through your house. Let me show you the difference between a series circuit and a parallel circuit.

Nat drew this picture:

Circuits

In order to have a complete circuit, electrons must flow from the negative terminial, throught the wires, and return to the positive terminal.

= dry cell   =bulb

Series Circuit

Each bulb adds more resistance, reducing the current.
If one bulb goes out, the circuit is broken, and all the bulbs go out.

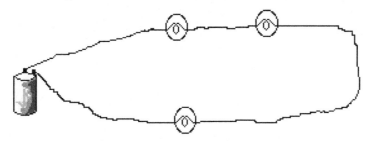

Parallel Circuit

Each new bulb adds an extra path for the electricty to travel through, increasing the current. If one bulb goes out, the others stay lit.

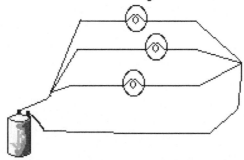

"Is science all you kids ever talk about?" asked Flame.

"It helps to understand things, if you know some science," said Nat. "When the doctor used electricity to shock Hector's heart, or when the doctor told us that Hector's corneas may be damaged, it pays to be able to understand what he was talking about."

"I am ignorant, when it comes to science," said Flame. "I feel I am at a big disadvantage because I don't know enough. I wish I knew more about science, so I could understand what is happening to my father."

Just then, Ann came back. "Hector's mother is with him," she said. "She was very upset that Hector got into a violent fight. She said that Hector was not very obedient: he doesn't always listen to his mother. She wanted to know why Nat lent Hector chemical equipment, but she doesn't want to have an argument. She just wants Hector to get better. She knows it will take time, but hopes for gradual improvement."

"I'm impatient," said Flame. "I want him to be better now!"

"We have to be patient," said Kate. "It will take some time for Hector to heal."

"I'm worried about his eyes," said Nat. "That acid was strong. Acid should only be used if it's diluted with water. How could I be so stupid to lend him my chemicals?"

"I want to see him," said Flame.

"Hector has ointment on both eyes, and they are covered with bandages," said Ann. "He can't see us."

"I hope he can see when they take the bandages off," said Kate.

"They are going to move Hector to a regular room in a moment or two," said Ann. "His mother said I could come back to visit him tomorrow.

"We're going with you," said Kate.

"At times like this, friends stick together," Nat added.

The Next day, Ann, Kate, Nat, and Flame went to the hospital together. They chipped in to buy a bunch of flowers.

"These flowers are beautiful," said Kate. "They smell so pretty."

"Isn't it lovely how plants make such pretty flowers for us to enjoy?" said Flame.

"Plants make flowers for themselves," said Nat. "Flowers are the reproductive organs of a plant. Flowers produce seeds, and seeds produce new plants."

"Do you mean to say that flowers have something to do with sexual reproduction?" asked Flame.

"That's what I'm saying," said Nat. "The flower is the sexual organ of the plant. Most flowers have both male and female sexual organs inside the flower. The stamen is the male sexual organ. The pistil is the female sexual organ.

Inner parts of flower

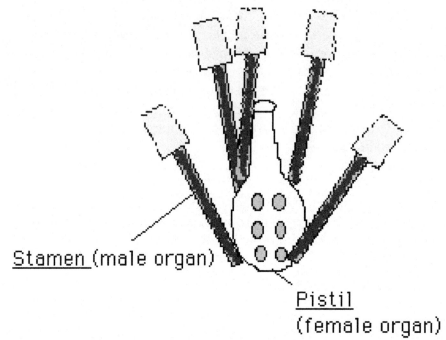

Stamen (male organ)

Pistil
(female organ)

Colored leaves called petals (not shown here)
surround these inner sexual organs of the flower.

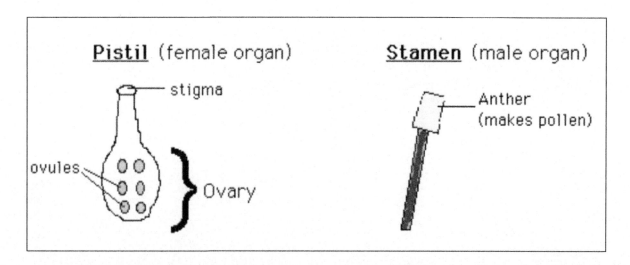

"The head of the stamen (anther) produces pollen. Each pollen grain produces a sperm nucleus. Ovules in the pistil produce egg cells. Bees bring pollen to the sticky stigma at the top of the pistil. A pollen tube grows down to each ovule. The sperm nucleus goes down the tube, and the sperm nucleus joins the egg nucleus. Each ovule grows into a seed, and the whole ovary becomes a fruit."

* * *

"Never mind the science lesson," said Kate. "Let's bring the flowers to Hector."

"We all can't all visit Hector at once," said Ann. "They won't let us all in. Let me go in first and bring him the flowers."

Hector was sitting up in his bed, when Ann walked in. He had a bandage on his head, and bandages covering both eyes. A piece of sausage and some cabbage sat on a plate.

"Hi," said Ann. "How are you feeling?"

"Who's there?" asked Hector. "Whose voice do I hear? I can't see with these bandages over my eyes."

"It's me, Ann. How are you doing?"

"I'm glad you came," said Hector. "I hate the food here "The breakfast had no bacon, and they gave me cabbage and sausage for supper. I wish I had a coke instead of milk for a beverage. The food here tastes like garbage."

Ann sat down on the bed next to Hector and held his hand.

"My head hurts," Hector said. "Why does my head hurt so much?"

"Bubba picked you up, turned you upside down, and dropped you head first onto a concrete step," said Ann. "You had a bad concussion. You almost died. Why did Bubba do that to you?"

"I have a confession to make," said Hector. "Do you remember when I was delivering medicine to a man who was dying from smoking cigarettes. He has a daughter."

"Yes," said Ann. "You said her name is Samantha."

"That *is* her name," said Hector, "but her nickname is Flame."

"Flame says she was with you at the concert" said Ann.

"I was" said Hector. "She bought two tickets for me and for her. I could not refuse. Then you said you had tickets, too. I didn't know what to do."

"How could you go out with her and lie to me?" asked Ann. "You know how much I dislike that girl."

"I'm sorry," said Hector. "Samantha is good looking, but you should know that you are the only one I love."

"Don't you think I'm good looking?" asked Ann.

"I do," said Hector. "You are cute and pretty. I just wish I could look at you now and see how beautiful you are, but I can't see! I can't wait for them to take these bandages off."

Just then, the doctor walked into the room.

"How are you feeling, today?" the doctor asked.

"My head hurts," said Hector.

"That's not unusual," said the doctor. "You had a pretty hard knock, young man. Your head should make gradual improvement. The pain should go away in a few days. Your visual problem is much more serious. We're going to take the bandages off your eyes, now. Keep your eyes closed until I take the bandages off and wash the ointment from your eyes."

When the doctor had finished removing the bandages and washing off the ointment, he said, "OK, now, open your eyes and let me have a look."

"I can't see! I can't see!," Hector cried. "It feels like I'm looking through wax paper. I can see some light, but no shapes."

The doctor looked at Hector's eyes.

"What's wrong?" Hector cried. "Why can't I see?"

"The cornea of each eye has been badly damaged from acid. The cornea is the clear outer covering of the eye. It should be transparent, completely clear like glass, allowing all light to go through. Right now your corneas are translucent, like wax paper. Some light can go through, but not in straight lines, so an image cannot be focused on the retina in the back of your eye."

"Will my eyes heal?" asked Hector? "My corneas will heal, and then I will see, right?"

"I'm sorry," said the doctor. "Your corneas cannot heal. Scar tissue may form, making each cornea opaque. Then, no light will get through. If we're lucky, some light will get through, so you will be able to tell the difference between day and night."

"If I'm *lucky*?!! If I'm *lucky*?!!! I want to be able to see the image of Ann's beautiful face again! I want to see my friends! I want to see the ocean, and the moon, and the stars over Orchard Beach again! I want to take the train to the Village and see all the sights of Manhattan. I want to take a voyage across the sea, or walk the open road and see America. What is the advantage of having eyes if they don't work anymore? I want to see! I want to see!" Hector began to cry. He was sobbing like a baby. Ann held him tight.

"I'm sure you will be able to see again," said Ann, trying to encourage Hector. "There must be something that can be done."

"There is one thing," said the doctor. "He could get a corneal transplant. Some people agree to give their organs for transplant when they die. If someone dies and donates his eyes to Hector, Hector could have his vision restored. In each eye, we remove Hector's damaged cornea, and replace it with the healthy cornea of a person that died. With a transplant, he has a fifty percent chance of seeing again, but there is a long waiting list. He could wait years for a transplant. But there is a significant chance that a transplant won't work. Each individual is different."

"Hector," said Ann, "have courage. I know you will be able to see again. Hang in there. You've got to be patient."

A nurse came in. "Visitors must leave, now," the nurse said. "The patients need their rest."

Ann went back to the waiting room, where the others were waiting.

"Hector can't see," she said. "His corneas are burned from the acid."

"It's all my fault," said Nat. "I should never have given him my chemistry set."

"I don't think a company would put concentrated acid in a chemistry set," said Kate.

"They don't," said Nat. "I ordered that on my own, pretending to be an adult."

"That was a stupid thing to do," said Flame.

"His only chance to see again is a corneal transplant," said Ann.

"Corneal transplant?" asked Flame.

"He needs to replace the cornea in each eye in order to see again," Ann replied. "He needs someone who is dying to donate his corneas for transplant."

"I want to see him," said Flame.

"They are not allowing visitors anymore," said Ann. "They will only allow his mother to see him later. We will have to come back tomorrow."

As they were about to leave the hospital, they saw an ambulance pull up. A man was wheeled into the emergency room.

"Hey!" shouted Flame. "That's my father!"

They all rushed to the emergency waiting room. Flame followed her father into the E.R.

"Daddy! Daddy!" cried Flame. "What's wrong?"

Flames father could hardly speak. Malignant tumors had grown in many parts of his body. His lungs were damaged from all the years of cigarette smoking. Increasing the dosage of his medication no longer helped. His body was not getting sufficient oxygen from his lungs. His muscles could not burn enough sugar because there was not enough oxygen. He was very weak. He could hardly speak, and his cancer had spread to his liver.

"Samantha, my beautiful girl," her father said. "I am dying from suffocation. I can't get enough air. The oxygen level of my blood is not sufficient to keep me alive. I have no energy. Cancer has stopped my liver from working right. Harmful chemicals are building up in my blood, and my liver can't fix the problem. I don't have much longer to live. Please don't make the mistake that I did as a teenager. Don't smoke. Stay away from drugs and alcohol. All that stuff is poison. Now I won't be able to see my little girl grow up and get married. I am sorry I have to leave you, my sweet daughter. I love you."

"No, Poppa! No!" cried Samantha. "I love you! Please don't leave me, Poppa!"

"That's the way it is," her father said. "We are given one life to live, and it should not be wasted by doing stupid things, like I did. Be good to other people. Help each other out. Show love to one another. That's what life is all about." Then he began to cough and could not talk.

After a few moments, he was able to speak again. "How's your friend, Hector, the delivery boy?"

"Poppa," Samantha said. "He's blind. There is damage to the cornea in each of his eyes. The only way he will ever be able to see again is if he has a corneal transplant. But there is a long waiting list for transplants."

Samantha's father thought for a moment. "I can do one last good deed before my departure from this world," he said. "I will sign a paper to give my corneas to your friend after I die. I have to die, but a child will be able to see again with the windows of my eyes."

* * *

The next day, while Samantha was home with her mother, an urgent call came from the hospital. Samantha and her mother rushed to the hospital. By the time they got there, Samantha's father was already dead. They rushed him to surgery. Samantha's father wanted to donate all his organs. His heart could not be transplanted because it was damaged from the chemicals in cigarette smoke. His liver had cancer and could not go to a man who had damaged his liver from heavy alcohol drinking. Because of the cancer, it wasn't safe to transplant his kidneys to a young girl who needed new kidneys to clean her blood by making urine. Only his corneas were safe for transplant, and they were going to Hector, who was waiting for them in the O.R. next door."

Ann, Nat, Kate, and Hector's mother all went to the funeral for Samantha's father. They all told Samantha and her mother what a wonderful thing Samantha's father had done. They all hoped that the transplant would work, and that Hector would see again, but there was an equal chance that it would not.

* * *

A few days later, Nat, Kate, Ann, and Samantha went to visit Hector. His eyes were covered with bandages, but under each bandage was a new cornea. The doctor and his assistant entered the room.

"Please step aside," the doctor said. "It is time to remove the bandages."

The assistant slowly took off each bandage, one at a time. He cleaned off the ointment from each eye. Then he said, "Open your eyes."

Hector slowly opened his eyes. "Ann, is that you?" he said. "I can see your beautiful face!" He looked around and said, "I can see Samantha, and Nat, and Kate! I can see! I can see! It is so magnificent to be able to see again!"

"You will be able to go home tomorrow," said the doctor. "You will have to come in every week to check your eyes, for a while, and every year for an annual checkup, but you should be fine."

Ann ran over to Hector and gave him a kiss. Then they all came over and hugged him.

Ann looked at Flame, the girl she had hated for so long. "Thank you for asking your father to donate his corneas to Hector. If not for you, Hector would still be blind."

"At least my father's death had some meaning," said Flame.

"Flame," said Ann, "you are really a kind person."

"You're not so bad yourself," Flame replied. "I am sorry I snapped on you so much over the years. I wasn't acting very mature."

"Flame, I was acting immature, too" said Ann.

"My good friends call me Samantha," Flame said.

"Samantha," said Ann. "I would like to be your friend, as long as you're not Hector's girlfriend."

"I don't think Hector can handle two girlfriends at a time," Samantha said. "Look what happened when he tried to handle more than one. Anyway, there's a new lifeguard at the beach that I have my eye on."

"Which lifeguard?" asked Kate.

"His name is Phil," Samantha replied.

"We know Phil," said Kate. "He smokes."

"I'll make him stop," said Samantha. "I can't stand the smell of cigarettes. Kids who smoke have bad breath. Even their clothing stinks. I'll tell Phil, if he wants me for his girlfriend, he has to give that junk up. And you know what — his kisses are a lot sweeter when he stops smoking.

* * *

A few weeks later, Hector, Ann, Nat, Kate, and Samantha were at the beach. The sun had set, and they were looking at the night sky.

"It's so nice to be able to see the moon and the stars," said Hector. "I will never again take my vision for granted."

"I have a rap song for the occasion," said Nat.

"Let's hear it," said Hector.

"Here we are at the beach again,
Looking at the stars, and everyone's a friend,
But it's not long ago whren it just wasn't so,
We used to fight and snap at kids we didn't know.

Some people say that I'm just an intellectual,
But I'm here with my girl, and I'm feeling very sensual,
Looking at the stars and at every individual,
Asking how we got here makes me feel very spiritual.

Thank you for permission to talk about my vision,
Of how to stick together without fighting or division.
If you want to get along, just listen to my song,
Because peace is my passion, and friendship is my mission.

Hector had two dates to go to a show,
Sitting in both seats was a problem, you know,
One girlfriend at a time is the only way to go,
Or you'll be running back and forth, and miss the whole show.

Bubba dropped poor Hector at that terrible event,
Hector landed on cement and his head had a dent,
The worst thing that happened was the acid in his eyes,
But Samantha saved the day to everyone's surprise.
Before he passed away, her dad did something right,
He gave his eyes for transplant and restored Hector's sight.

Now, we've had a lot of fun, and we've all been very social,
The summers almost over, and soon it'll be official,
But before I say goodbye, one thing is very crucial,
One special thing to learn, and this isn't a commercial.

If someone starts with you, be strong and walk away,
Keep away from a fight, and live another day.
It takes a lot of courage just to do what I say,
But making peace with each other — that's the only way.

Thanks for listening to my song,
You've all been very patient,

I hope you learn to get along,
And live until you're ancient.

Don't snap on each other,
On your sister or your brother,
Have compassion for each other,
Learn to love one another.
Love your father and your mother,
Live in peace with your brother,
Make your life a great adventure,
And be in harmony with nature.

 "I liked that," said Kate.
 "Me too," said Hector. "Let's form a circle."
 Hector, Ann, Nat, Kate, and Samantha gathered together in a circle. They put their right hands together and shouted,

"Friends forever!"

Comprehension Questions

1. What is a pulse?

2. How was Hector's heart made to beat again?

3. What is voltage?

4. What is electric current?

5. What does resistance do to the amount of current flowing through a wire?

6. What has more resistance — a thick wire or a thin wire?

7. Given the same voltage, which will have more current — a thick wire or a thin wire?

8. Draw a battery and four bulbs in a series circuit.

9. Draw a battery and four bulbs in a parallel circuit.

10. A bulb burned out in Ann's living room. The other bulbs stayed on. What kind of circuit does Ann have in her living room?

11. A bulb burned out on Kate's Christmas tree, and the other bulbs went out. Her Christmas lights are wired with a _____ circuit.

12. Why do plants produce flowers?

13. What is the male organ of the flower?

14. What is the female organ of the flower?

15. What is an ovule?

16. An ovule can grow into a _____.

17. The ovary of the flower will grow into a _____.

18. How was Hector's vision restored?

19. Why is emphysema a bad disease?

20. Give three reasons why it is bad to smoke.

21. What good deed did Flame's father do before he died?

22. Why won't Flame go out with boys who smoke?

23. Why did Ann and Flame become friends, in the end?

Printed in Great Britain
by Amazon

27938294R00051